Recognizing God's Fingerprints

Miracles of Rescue, Reset and Rejoicing

Susan Ceraldi Jaquith

 Inscript

I dedicate this book to my husband Robert E. Jaquith, one of the greatest miracles of my life.
And posthumously to Berthe L. Gagne and Father William Dudack, who repaired and mentored me over the years, free of charge, with patience and love.

Other Books by Author

Scraps from the Father's Banquet Table:
Spiritual Food for Thought

Contents

Author's Note

This book, although it describes some key events that happened in my life, is not an autobiography or a complete story of my life.

It is not about anything that I did or didn't do; right or wrong, good or bad. It is about what God chose to do for me at times when I needed Him most, or when He chose to do something through me for someone else in need. God did these things because of who He is, not because of who I am or fail to be.

And He left His fingerprints along the way.

Introduction

I rewrote this introduction after completing the first draft of this book, which is typical, because it is easier to write an introduction after gaining a better understanding of how the book evolved during its creation. My initial vision and desire for this book was to document the more memorable times in my life when I knew beyond all doubt that God had intervened on my behalf. I did not want to forget such moments, especially as I get older, and I also thought sharing such moments could be of some benefit to others when they read about these encounters. My plan was to create the most positive book ever! I thought it would be my perfect life story without all the bad things that of course happened in between these wonderful and wonder-filled moments. This book was initially envisioned to be a beautiful collection of only mountaintop experiences!

What I quickly learned as I wrote one entry after another was that most often the miraculous moment that I intended to write about did not make sense, or could not be appreciated, without first putting it into the context of the life situation at the time God intervened. I decided that I would need to include information about the context of the miraculous moment I was describing. When I began to do that, I inevitably found myself having to share much more about the painful or dark event that preceded the miracle. Although my intent for this book was to skip over such negative circumstances, I realized that I needed to tell their story as well in order for the miracle to be grasped.

For Christians, this should come as no surprise, because we know that we could not have the power and joy of the Easter resurrection of Jesus without His Good Friday crucifixion. The experience of writing this book has made me realize how often I would prefer to take Jesus off His cross - and take myself and those I love off our crosses as well – even with the knowledge that resurrection lies ahead. So, I began to see that those dark times were often the backdrop for these encounters with light in my life, and that in order to really be able to see the brightness of His light and power at work in my life, I could not separate the miracles from the struggles that made God's help so necessary (and appreciated).

I recall a statement, but do not know who said it, that "God is always with us and strengthens us to endure our life's trials; but every once in a while, He does 'part the Red Sea' in our circumstance." Considering my realization that I could not describe these miraculous moments without first explaining the trials that preceded them, I thought more about Moses and the Red Sea. If God had simply parted the Red Sea for Moses and the Israelites to cross over, yes, that would still have been quite a miraculous moment, but it loses some of its "miraculous-ness" when you forget that it happened after the Israelites were being chased by Pharaoh's chariots and charioteers that were intent on killing them! They were running for their lives from their persecutors and found themselves up against the Red Sea with a vicious army at their heels! It is then that God intervened on their behalf. It is interesting to me that they first had to endure being abused by their Egyptian masters, had to flee, and run, and go through the trial of escape before the miracle was given to them as a pure gift and miraculous intervention. This is clearly symbolic of so much of our own lives.

There is another aspect to miracles that I discovered during the writing of this book, and that is the ordinariness of some miracles. In such cases, the Red Sea was not parted before my eyes, but the grip on me from current difficult circumstances, or my past, was. Something oppressive was either lifted, healed and/or transformed during God's intervention. Conversely, on occasion, some of my experiences did transcend ordinariness, but for the most part, what I consider to be God's miraculous work has been done through everyday people and situations, often in response to my prayers for His help.

Then there were those times when the miracles seemed to be God's reassurance of His presence with me in my life. Rather than answering my question at hand or handing out an instant solution for me to grab onto, He chose instead to give me a sign of His presence with me amid my circumstance. In these miracles, somehow, God found a way to convey to me that He heard my prayer, tasted my tears, saw the injustices done to me, or was aware of the sweetness of one of my acts of kindness toward another. Sometimes God intervenes so intimately and so specifically that we know beyond all doubt that He is with us, and really does know exactly how many hairs are on our heads as the Bible says: "Indeed, the very hairs on your head are numbered." (Luke 12:7).

In the adorable Winnie the Pooh cartoon shown below, the quote from Hans Christian Anderson states "The whole world is a series of miracles, but we are so used to them we call them ordinary things." Perhaps a miracle, or a miraculous moment, then, is one of the most natural of all of life's moments.

This book is like a spiritual charm bracelet for me; each testimony commemorating a special moment where I knew beyond all doubt that God intervened in my life when I most needed Him to. In terms of the book's structure, I first present my miracle story and then ask

"The whole world is a series of miracles, but we're so used to them we call them ordinary things."

(Hans Christian Andersen)

Image: A. A. Milne

the question: "What about your story?" The vision I have for this book is to not only share the wonderful things I have seen God do in my life, but also to invite you to connect with your own miracle stories and realize God's fingerprints on your life.

May this book be a blessing to you, my reader, and help you to allow God into your deepest, most honest inner self; and dare to believe in and take comfort in His love for you. That is when the miraculous hand of God is the freest to intervene in our lives, leaving His fingerprints of miracles of rescue, reset and rejoicing.

On Being Born

As I begin this entry, I am hearing the show tune in my head from the 1959 Rogers and Hammerstein musical "The Sound of Music, "Do-Re-Mi"; and the words so beautifully sung by Julie Andrews… "let's start at the very beginning, a very good place to start…when we read we begin with A B C, when we sing we begin with Do- Re- Mi…". So, I decided to make the first chapter of the book to be about my birth. This decision put me on the course of presenting the other miracle accounts chronologically. This approach offered the additional benefit of seeing the way God intervened in my life over time. Of course, I believe that every birth is a miracle of God, not just my own. So, when you read this entry, please keep in mind that I do not think of this as just my miracle story. My husband has often said, in awe, that the science required for any one of us to be conceived and born involves miracles we may not fully realize. The chances of that precise sperm surviving the journey to fertilize the precise egg that is viable for a time, that will eventually become "me," is nothing short of a miracle.

Before I tell you my "being born" story, I want to share the miracle of how my parents first met. I realize it is their miracle story, not mine, but let's just say I "inherited it," and because of their miracle, I came to be. Prior to my parents meeting, my mother lived in East Hartford,

CT and my father lived in Windsor, CT. My mother was the sixth of seven children, and my father was the youngest of four. As is the custom in high school, after my mother had her class yearbook picture taken, she gave out wallet sized pictures to some of her girlfriends and family. As their story goes, her older sister Peggy who worked at Singer Sewing Machine gave my mother's picture to her co-worker girlfriend. I am not sure why her friend wanted my mother's picture, but she took it and kept it in her wallet. Later she was with a friend of hers, a young man named Ray from Windsor, who saw the picture and had the audacity to ask if he could have it! Also surprising to me is that she would give my mother's picture to a guy my mother did not even know! This was back in the 1940's so etiquette and privacy concerns may not have been as they are today.

Well, it turned out that Ray happened to be a classmate of my future father. At one point when my father and Ray were together, my father asked him if he had change for a $2 bill. Ray took out his wallet to give him change, and my father saw my mother's pretty face smiling back at him. It was love at first sight for my dad, and he fell head over heels in love with her via her picture! My father asked Ray "who is this girl?" The guy pretended that he knew my mother, said that she was just a girl he knew. My father asked him for my mother's phone number, which of course he did not have, but he later got it for my father from the co-worker at Singer who got it from my Aunt Peggy.

Smitten as he was, my father made a cold phone call to the pretty girl in the picture from East Hartford, who a few years later would become his wife, my mother! He told her on that first call that someday he was going to marry her. Apparently, she giggled and kept talking to him. Mom was fifteen and Dad was seventeen at the time of the call. I can't help but think that another real miracle here is that she did not hang up on him! They proceeded to have a phone courtship for many months, and then finally after my mother turned sixteen, they were allowed to plan a date at the movie theater accompanied by my mother's three older sisters! Three years later they were married; my mother was nineteen and my father was twenty-one years old. As of this writing, they are still going strong at 93 and 95 years old, married 74 years.

In our family history, particularly on my mother's side, being able to conceive, carry and deliver a baby was not always a given, with infertility and miscarriages at a frequency that defied the odds. My mother conceived twice before her pregnancy with me, however, she had two miscarriages well into both of those pregnancies. Back in the 1950's, there was a lot more trial and error with hormone therapies than there is now, not only to help with conception issues, but also for the prevention of miscarriages. My mother took a hormone regimen to be able to carry me full term. Because of her insatiable longing to have children (my father had given up after the second miscarriage and did not want my mother, or himself, to suffer another such loss) she insisted on trying again. She was able to carry me full term.

I was successfully delivered by C-section on August 3, 1956. Throughout my life I was told repeatedly by my parents, especially at each one of my birthdays when they called to sing to me, that I was their miracle baby. I was welcomed into the most loving arms possible. I was wanted and cherished and yes, overprotected; I might have even been loved too much if there could ever be such a thing. In fact, we were such a lovely family of three that I had a bit of an emotional adjustment three years later when my sister was born as to why we needed anyone else! My sister's birth was another miracle in their lives, and as I would later come to realize and cherish, a miracle in mine as well.

On every one of my birthdays, I celebrate the miracle of my birth and my parents' perseverance to continue to choose life; I do not celebrate it because of any narcissistic belief that I think I am so great, but rather because I truly believe that my life, and yours, have a God given meaning and purpose in the time that we have been placed. So, on your birthday, I invite you to do the same, regardless of the circumstances of your conception. Celebrate the miracle of your birth and the number of days you have been given with which to leave your fingerprints on planet earth.

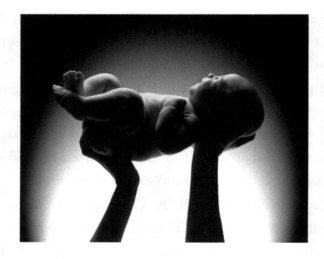

What About Your Story?

How do you feel when your birthday rolls around?

Who typically celebrates your birthday with you?

What makes you feel special on your birthday?

I think that God celebrates your birthday, even if no one else does.

And He is aware of your life every day, from "womb to tomb."

1. As I get older - well not as for children i was younger - BUT Know GOD has given me another yer with my family - Very Very Blessd

2. Husband - Kids - mom

3. My family

4. yes I know he does - aske is still gone me life here.

5.

On Being Born Again

Equally precious to me as my natural birthday is the day that I was "born again." Now, I can almost see your eyes rolling, and I can appreciate what you might be thinking, because these words are so overused or misused, that they can hardly convey the true meaning of this moment in a person's life. It is hard to get past the lingo that turns people off, and I wish I could find the right words to convey the moment and its power to heal and transform a life. Let me simply say that the day you discover God's love for you, and the fact that He sent His Son Jesus to die to set you free, and then respond to that by making a deliberate decision to accept His love, is like a birthday of your own choosing, and your life will never be the same. It is one of those miracles of rescue, reset and rejoicing, all in one. Here is how my special moment happened.

When I was fourteen years old, I had my young teenage girl's heart broken by a boyfriend that I thought for sure was "the one." I honestly do not know how teenagers survive these years, except by the grace of God. To complicate my saga, I was friends with this boy's sister, and still wanted to remain friends with her. She knew I was hurting and invited me to attend a movie with her at the Newington Theater. She told me it was a comedy, and that it would cheer me up. I thought that would be a good idea, so I decided to go. It was a comedy all right…

one of God's greatest jokes...for lo and behold we realized we were at a Billy Graham movie called "For Pete's Sake." Because the movie was being shown in my town's *"normal"* movie theater, you can better understand how I could have been surprised to find myself at a Billy Graham movie, which at that time I would not have agreed to go see.

I could not believe we had to sit through such a movie! It wasn't funny at all. As I recall, the movie was about a woman that became a believer in Jesus and began to pray and read the Bible. Her husband, however, scoffed at her newfound faith. Her Bible, as well as her reading of it, was visible in their home. One day the woman was on a stepladder doing something in the house while the husband was not home, and she fell off the ladder and eventually died from her injuries. He came home to find her on the floor, and was devastated, blaming himself for not having been there to help her, and thinking, rightly or wrongly, that he could have saved her life. He loved her and was torn with grief and guilt.

One day, well after her funeral, his eyes were drawn to her Bible on the nightstand, and he opened it and began to read certain passages she had highlighted as her favorite passages. Because of his sorrow, he had a new open space in his heart and wanted to know what meant so much to his wife in these writings. He also had a desire to find comfort in God's love for himself in his grief. He heard about a Billy Graham crusade that was scheduled to be held close to where he lived and decided to attend. Long story short, he went forward during the altar call and accepted Jesus into his life as his Lord and Savior.

At that point in the movie, I was choked up and moved by the man's loss, grief, and guilt. I cried at the end, grateful that he found Jesus, but not really understanding what that meant, especially the words "accept Jesus as your personal Lord and Savior."

As the credits were rolling, someone went on the stage in the movie

7

theater to a microphone and invited anyone in the theater that wanted to accept Jesus as their personal Lord and Savior to come forward. Again, I really did not understand what I was being asked, except that he said it was about being forgiven and finding and entering into a personal relationship with Jesus through prayer. All I knew was that I wanted that - a personal relationship with Jesus - whatever it was, and I needed to feel God close to me. I realized that there was such an emptiness and hurt in my heart, and a longing for more of God. Still without full understanding, and on pure impulse, I found myself walking forward to the front of the theater to accept Jesus. The leaders read a prayer that we were told to recite if we wanted to invite God into our heart. It is called "The Sinner's Prayer," and Billy Graham made it famous:

> "Dear Lord Jesus, I know I am a sinner, and I ask for Your forgiveness. I believe You died for my sins and rose from the dead. I turn from my sins and invite You to come into my heart and life. I want to trust and follow You as my Lord and Savior. Amen."

Those of us that came forward were then invited to give our name and phone number (there was no email back then!) if we wanted to learn more and be contacted. I gave my name and number, again not sure what this was about or what it would lead to. They also gave us a small New Testament and suggested we start by reading the Gospel of John to begin to get to know who Jesus was. To my surprise I had a genuine desire to read it and I started that night.

I still did not connect the dots and realize that the New Testament was the second half of the Bible, and that the Gospels were the first part of the New Testament. I did not realize I was really reading the Bible because my perception of the Bible was a big black book full of words that no one could ever understand. We always had a family

Bible on our coffee table, the one my father received when he was in the Marines, but as good pre-Vatican II Catholics at the time, we were not supposed to open it to read and interpret it for ourselves; rather, we were to rely on the church's teachings and sermons at mass. As I read the gospels, I was surprised to discover that the readings were those that I had heard on Sunday at mass. I had never quite realized that the readings we listened to were from the Bible.

True to their word, a few days later I received a phone call from a young woman who lived in my town. She told me about a Bible study that met in her home, and she invited me to attend. My mother was delighted that I wanted to attend a Bible study instead of a party with a bad crowd, or mope around over a boyfriend, so she eagerly drove me to it. My father, on the other hand, was a loyal Catholic so we had to pretend that I was going to a party and not a Protestant Bible Study!!! How funny is that!

My parents saw that I was starting to perk up and be happy again. They saw a change in me. I began to be drawn to the Bible, and I could not wait to continue reading it. I wanted to learn more about Jesus. Not about church, or denominations, or theology, but about Jesus especially when He was on the earth as a man.

I eagerly began reading the Gospels. The very last verses at the end of Matthew's gospel grabbed my heart when Jesus said these words to His apostles, and to each of us now:

> Matthew 28:19-20: "Go therefore and make disciples of all the nations, baptizing them in the name of the Father and the Son and the Holy Spirit, teaching them to observe all that I commanded you; and lo, I am with you always, even to the end of the age."

That promise of Jesus to be with us always, even to the end of time, were the most comforting words I had ever heard. I realized that I am never alone. When we whisper His name, Jesus, He really is as close to us as our very breath.

After I finished reading the four gospels, I began reading Acts of the Apostles (also called the Book of Acts). It is a book that documents the life of the apostles after Jesus returned to heaven. I was quite taken aback when I first read in the Book of Acts that the apostle Peter could heal people, just like Jesus did! I never knew that! Acts of the Apostles also says that the crowds gathered around when Peter passed by because even his shadow healed them when he passed by them!

I also read this account in Acts 3:6-10 that changed me. It was when Peter and John were on their way to the temple and they passed by a paralytic beggar, who was asking for alms:

> [6] Then Peter said, Silver and gold have I none; but such as I have give
> I thee: In the name of Jesus Christ of Nazareth rise up and walk.
> [7] And he took him by the right hand and lifted him up: and im-
> mediately his feet and ankle bones received strength."

I could not believe that the man was instantly healed, and obediently stood up and walked! My mind could not process this new information! This triggered so many questions in my mind such as "why don't we ever hear about or even know about all the miracles the disciples were able to do in Acts of the Apostles when we are in church?" We only hear about the miracles Jesus did in the Gospels. And then an even greater question emerged within me: "Why do I not see these healings happening in church today?"

I can't recall where I heard this account about when St. Thomas Aquinas first went to Rome and saw the Cystine chapel, his Vatican guide pointed out the beautiful gold and the artwork in the chapel. The guide said, "No longer can we say silver and gold have I none."

And St. Thomas said, "Neither can you say Rise Up and Walk."

I am disappointed to say that this fervor of mine continued for a year and then began to wane when I began a new relationship during my junior year of high school. I slowly slid back into caring more about peers and romance than continuing down the path I had found. But I could never forget what I had experienced, and my newfound deeper faith, especially enkindled when reading the Bible. Although my teenage girl commitment to the Lord was shallow, my love for Jesus was nevertheless very real, and I could never deny, or wish to deny, all that I had learned. I was to come back to Jesus again, a few years later, in full force and with a full heart and a more stable commitment. But I suppose I must have needed to make a few more mistakes first. In the following chapters you will see that He was faithful to continue to pursue me, despite my lapses, as promised in His Word from Philippians 1:6:

> [6] being confident of this, that he who began a good work in you will carry it on to completion until the day of Christ Jesus.

It was not until five years later that I would learn about the gifts of the Holy Spirit described by St. Paul in 1 Corinthians 12, and experience healing ministries in our day and age through the Holy Spirit. It made sense to me that miracles would still happen, because why would God not want to continue the ministry of Jesus through Holy Spirit-filled believers in our generation? And the Bible says, "Jesus Christ is the same, yesterday, today and forever." Why would we think that miracles would cease?

Getting back to the miraculous moment (or moments) that I am writing about in this chapter…the miracle to me was God's ability to get me to a Billy Graham movie in the first place, give me the courage to go forward in the movie theater and ask Jesus to come into my heart, then provide my name to be contacted, and find a way to get me to a Protestant bible study in town, where they put a readable Bible into my hands that I would have and cherish every day of my life going forward.

John 3:16-17:

[16] For God so loved the world that He gave His only begotten Son, that whoever believes in Him should not perish but have everlasting life. [17] For God did not send His Son into the world to condemn the world, but that the world through Him might be saved.

What About Your Story? *yes* OH

Have you had a "being born again" miracle moment? If so, recall the details and how you felt when you realized that God loved not only the whole world, but YOU and that He wanted a personal relationship with you.

If you cannot recall such a moment, or never made a conscious decision to accept Jesus as your Savior, it helps to consider a few questions that may help you realize your need for Jesus such as: Is there something you don't like but cannot change about yourself, such as a destructive tendency or pattern of bad behavior that you can't seem to stop on your own, no matter how hard you try?

- Do you have a propensity toward anger, lying, hating, hiding, or an uncontrollable addiction to drugs or alcohol, or even addictions to persons that you cannot get free from? *Not Any More*
- Do you feel an emptiness within that nothing is able to fill? *No*
- Do you lack a sense of inner peace or feel distant from God? *No*
- Did you ever wish that someone could just come in and "fix you?" *GOD HAS!!*

There is someone…you have such a Savior, and His name is Jesus!

If you recognize such needs in yourself, then dare to take the next step and ask Jesus to come into your life and be your Lord and Savior. Ask Him to reveal Himself to you.

Now is the time! Jump in with both feet!

A Dream about a Gold Cross

I have a friend who writes essays, Bill Dunn, and he once wrote that "dreams are like movies that always star me!" I love that description of our dreams! There were periods of time when I was fascinated with my dreams and wondered what they meant. I knew that the symbols in my dreams had meaning and were somehow chosen by my brain to communicate some truth, but even though I tried writing them down, I was never able to decipher their code.

What also intrigued me was the notion that God often spoke to His people through their dreams, as recorded many times, particularly in the Old Testament. For example, Jacob's son, Joseph, and Daniel were both given the gift of dreams, and interpreting dreams, and this gift saved their lives. In the Gospel we hear several accounts of Joseph's dreams: he was told in a dream that it was "ok" to take Mary, who was pregnant, as his wife; after Jesus was born, he was warned in a dream to take the child (Jesus) and His mother to Egypt.

Most of the time our brains tell us a story using images in our dreams, and the images chosen by our brain can be symbolic rather than literal. More often than not, we cannot understand them, or they do not make any sense, but if you start paying attention to them, typically by writing them down in a journal, you can begin to see some repeat symbols that your brain often chooses to use to represent someone or something. We often notice we have repetitive dreams, e.g., in my dreams I often find a surprise extra room in my house – one that I never knew was there, but one that had always been there, yet I had never discovered it. Another repeat dream I have is of me holding a baby. I often have that dream when I am considering something new in my life, e.g., a new book, a new venture, a new home, etc.

In real life I have one sibling, my younger sister Judy. We joke about being each other's favorite sister. We grew up in a Cape style home, and we each had our own bedroom upstairs with a shared bathroom in between. The dream about the gold cross that I am writing about in this chapter took place in the upstairs area of our house. To this day, I recall this dream, and no interpretation is needed to understand its meaning as it was pretty clear.

In the dream I was wearing a simple gold cross necklace, and it was appropriately sized for my height and build. It was meaningful to me in the dream, and I would put my hand on it to touch it and appreciate that I had it to wear. I was wearing it all the time and it was a focal point – the dream kept "showing it" to me. In my dream my sister and I had a big fight about something, and I cannot even recall what the fight was about. But I became angrier and angrier, and the angrier I became, the smaller the cross on my necklace became. Then at one point I totally lost my temper and shouted at my sister and stomped away, heading back to my bedroom, and loudly slamming my door. Once in my room, I put my hand up to my necklace and suddenly discovered that the necklace had disappeared! It was completely gone.

Still in the dream, I was grieved by the loss of the necklace, and I clearly knew that I was in the wrong. I slowly opened my bedroom door and walked across the hallway (which seemed to be many miles long!) to my sister's bedroom. I went into her room and told her I was sorry, and we hugged. It seemed like an exceedingly long walk because

15

the walk to forgiveness is always a difficult journey to make, choosing to apologize rather than to go to bed angry and stay angry. When I then turned back to return to my own bedroom, not only had the cross necklace returned to my neck, but the cross was huge! It was as tall as I was! I could hardly walk with it draped around my neck and it was glistening!

I have never forgotten that dream. It taught me several lessons, the obvious one being about saying I am sorry when I have hurt someone. Even if I did not cause the argument, and I cannot recall in the dream who or what caused the argument, if I lose my temper and begin shouting, then I have entered a place that warrants an apology from me.

The second lesson I learned is what Ephesians 4:26-27 teaches: "In your anger do not sin": Do not let the sun go down while you are still angry, and do not give the devil a foothold."

The third lesson I learned was about the hypocrisy of looking like a Christian, talking the talk, wearing the right jewelry, but without really living the faith. We are called to walk the walk in those day-to-day moments that challenge us to choose love over anger.

What About Your Story?

Is there someone you need to apologize to? Ask God to show you.

Do you recall a dream that stayed with you because it seemed to carry a message or a teaching for you? If so, pray for the understanding of your dream. You might try journaling about it so you can come back to it at a later time.

Ask God to give you the gift of a spiritual dream when your mind and life seems so cluttered you feel like you cannot even connect to God in prayer. Sometimes a dream can break through, bringing insights from your subconscious to your conscious mind, where you can possibly take actions based on new understanding of your circumstances.

1. Not an apology for any wrong doing;
But not seen or calling Charette;
I lee Lee serviece and I
Can't seem to see her in the here —
I need strenght to call a list ——

Making the "Basketball Honor Roll"

First, allow me to put this entry in perspective for you. I am not very athletic, and never was. I was overweight as a child – from third grade to eighth grade - and that was a source of much pain and humiliation during my school years. Add to that, I had to wear glasses from 4 years old until I was 12 (we are talking bifocals for several of those years), and if that wasn't enough, I needed braces in the fifth grade. My school photos over the years were not the best.

At the end of eighth grade, from April through June, I managed to lose twenty pounds by a self-imposed diet. I did this after a Sadie Hawkins school dance, when the boy I had a crush on found out I liked him, was surprised that he was my secret crush, and of course did not feel the same way about me. During the summer of 1970 I continued to lose another ten pounds and returned to school as a freshman in high school at a normal and attractive weight. It was quite a victory in my life!

As life would have it, on Labor Day weekend, two days before the first day of high school, I managed to break my nose while doing a back-flip diving off a chair (there was no diving board) into our family's brand new inground swimming pool. When I did my flip, my feet accidentally kicked the chair too far out behind me (it was a perfect flip, I might add), resulting in my face hitting the side of the pool instead of the water. So, I entered my first year of high school at an awesome weight, in a brand-new red dress bought especially for the occasion of showing off my tiny new waistline - but with 2 horrendous black eyes and a huge nose!

As a student, I excelled academically, and this became especially apparent during senior year in high school when I was shocked to learn that I had achieved a class rank of 3 out of my class of 459 students. I also had a part-time administrative assistant job after school from 3 to 5 p.m. Monday through Friday, thanks to my father who called all his customer contacts the week before I turned sixteen to ask if any of them would be willing to hire a part-time student. While my school friends were joining clubs that met after school, sports teams, and the like, I had a job to get to, and immediately left school after the last bell to get to Hartford by 3 o'clock. Although I missed out on a lot of the social bonding that happens with after-school activities, I did enjoy having some of my "own money" to spend on new skinny clothes and entertainment that were beyond what was required of a parent to provide. Turns out I was a great typist too. I have always said typing was my most important class in school. Not to mention the side benefit of the trouble I did not get into because I was too busy working!

I was always on the honor roll so belonged to the National Honor Society. During our senior year, the National Honor Society sponsored a "fun evening" – a faculty vs. National Honor Society student basketball game. To add to the fun, we had to come to the game and play basketball dressed in costume! I decided to go as a black cat because I love cats. I easily made a pretty cute looking costume, complete with ears, whiskers, a pink nose, and a nice tail if I say so myself.

The big night came, and I was stressed out because I am not an athlete. I just did not want to embarrass myself in front of my teachers, classmates, and parents in the bleachers. My strategy was to run up and down the court and simply try to blend in. I had flashbacks of memories of never being picked to be on a team. It was always heart wrenching standing there waiting for my name to be called, to be picked, and hear the whispers ("oh, I hope we don't get stuck with her on our team"). I would find some happiness when I was the second to the last person picked, but the humiliation was fierce. I sure hope physical education teachers have a better way of having students form their teams nowadays. Some of my NHS classmates were very excited about this game because they had the chance to show they could be both athletic and smart. So, these students were playing somewhat "cutthroat" on the basketball court.

I am not sure where the miracle began, but at some point, someone stepped on my tail while I was dribbling the ball, causing me to stumble, which the referee called and awarded me not one, but *two* foul shots! I was so nervous, and excited, and was trembling, because I soon realized I had to stand on the foul line, ALONE, and take my two shots. All eyes were on me - my worst possible scenario for the evening. I bounced the ball (to buy more time), aimed carefully, and lo and behold I got the first shot in!! The thrill of success and the sound of applause was amazing, but not nearly as great as the relief I felt knowing that even if I missed the next shot, I had already scored a point for my team. What came next was miracle number two! On my second shot I made another basket!!! Can you imagine my joy? I had never known before in my life the sound of cheering and clapping for me because of my athletic accomplishments! I still feel the adrenaline flowing as I relive that moment.

As if that was not enough, the next miracle occurred when by the end of the game, which was at least another quarter after my two foul shots, the student team won the game by two points!!! I still to this day like to imagine that I won the game for my team!!!

But there is another miracle that prepared me for the miraculous moment I just described. When I was growing up, my sister and I lived next door to our cousins who were both boys. They had a basketball hoop at the beginning of their single car width driveway, and we would play games like "round the clock" where you would shoot from different clock number locations around a circle and try to get a basket. Although I was not a fast runner or very aggressive, I enjoyed those foul shots where you did not have to try to get the ball away from anyone, or run up and down the court, or compete with anyone but yourself. I think the Lord had me training for that one miraculous moment in high school that would heal a thousand other moments!

Getting back to my thrilling basketball game, there was even one more gift from the Lord in this story. The photographer at the Honor Society Basketball Game snapped a picture of me dribbling the ball down the court before I was fouled, and that picture ended up being included in our high school yearbook supplement, with yet another oddity…the picture appears on page 217 of the Sequin 1974 Newington High School yearbook, but the page numbers are out of sequence. The pages go from page 214, then to page 217, then to page 215, and then ending with page 216. This was so fitting to me in that my "victory" on the basketball court was truly a page out of time!

It was so kind of God to put His finishing touches on this precious moment of healing and joy in my life by having it captured in a photograph and preserved for all time. That moment far overrode the history of some difficult past moments that came before my miraculous moment on the high school basketball court.

What About Your Story?

Do you have a childhood "stigma" – a lie you are still buying into about yourself that comes from a childhood insult or wound, e.g., feelings of being inadequate, inferior, a loser, a failure...

Ask the Lord to come into that moment when your inner child was hurt whether by words spoken or attacks on your person. See Him stand between you and the person who hurt you. Hear Him say that you are God's child, created for a unique purpose, and gifted to become who you were meant to be...who you long to be.

Using your imagination, watch what Jesus can do to transform that painful moment and replace the lies you believe about yourself with the truth of His love for you and the promise that He has a good plan for your life.

Palm Sunday 1977

The experience I am documenting in this chapter was the most difficult one for me to write, because it put me on a path that defined the rest of my life, and it was a turning point in my life. It comes under the category of "that which cannot be described with words." It happened when I was a college student in my junior year, attending mass on Palm Sunday (1977) at our university chapel, Goddard Chapel. I will first provide you some context of my life at the time …a "you are here" map if you will.

I graduated high school in 1974 and went away to college, Tufts University, with the goal of becoming a math teacher. Because of my class rank, my high school guidance counselor strongly advised me to go to college. Up until then I had not given it a moment's thought. I knew that my grades were consistently quite good, but for me, I was just trying to do my best. I did not have a future goal or plan in mind. Because my guidance counselor was so passionate about my future, and so intent on helping me define my choices and the next steps I should be taking, I followed the advice given and applied to six different colleges. My family was not wealthy, so affordability was an important consideration. As it turned out, I was able to go to Tufts University because of the scholarships and financial aid that I was offered. Again, as life played out, my high school boyfriend also got accepted to Tufts, so it seemed to me going to Tufts was a logical next step. I was comfortable knowing that I would not be completely alone when going away to college, and that we would not have to consider or embark on a long-distance relationship. I was not ready for that much change in my life all at once.

Both of us were raised as Catholics, so we attended Sunday mass almost regularly at the campus chapel. Particularly during final exam time, it really seemed like a wise thing to do to make sure we were in God's good graces. Attending the Sunday mass was also a pleasant social event, as it was followed by brunch with friends.

The Passion of Christ is always read completely on Palm Sunday at Catholic mass. I cannot remember when exactly, but at some point the Catholic Church proclaimed the Passion gospel by assigning readers for each person in the gospel account; it was read like a play rather than having one priest or deacon read the entire account, which takes longer than typical Sunday gospel readings. The priest always reads the words spoken by Jesus, and another reader reads the part of the Narrator, and the other "characters" in the gospel account are also assigned. Those of us in the pews are asked to read out loud together the part of the "Crowd."

On this Palm Sunday in 1977, as I read my part as a member of the Crowd, I began to feel a pervasive deep pang in my heart when it came to saying the words I had to say. When Pilate asked, "who should I release to you, this Jesus of Nazareth, or Barabbas?" we had to shout "Barabbas." Barabbas was a convicted criminal. Then Pilate asks the crowd, the same crowd that days before threw Palm branches along Jesus's path hailing Him as their King, "then what shall I do with Jesus of Nazareth?" We the Crowd had to read the words "Crucify Him, Crucify Him." (Matthew 27:21). By then I was all choked up and I found that I just could not say those words. Something happened. I was no longer listening to a reading, or even reading a reading; rather, I was now in the reading and in the crowd. I could even smell the sweat of the crowd, and I could see Jesus. I now know it was the Holy Spirit that transported me to this moment in time via my imagination.

I felt as if Jesus was someone I knew, like a family member; someone close to me that was going to be killed. I knew that He was good, and even more gripping, I knew that He was INNOCENT. I felt frantic to try to find a way to stop this "mistake." I wept silently and wondered why I had never felt or thought of this before. I realized in a new way how savagely beaten He was even before being crucified, seeing in my mind's eye His wounds oozing with blood and sweat dripping and burning into those wounds.

The realization that the person being killed was the Son of God blew my mind. I remembered the Christmas story, the miracle of Jesus's conception by the Holy Spirit, and His human birth from a virgin mother, Mary. They did not know who they were about to put to death! And the realization of how Jesus spent His life loving, healing, teaching, performing miracles and delivering people from evil overwhelmed me. Why would we want to stop this man Jesus from continuing to do those marvelous works on our behalf as long as He possibly could?

I hated that it was God that they were killing. God!!!! Why would anyone want to stop God from continuing to love, heal and teach us? I then clearly saw the hands of Jesus about to be nailed - hands that healed the sick and worked miracles, being nailed to the cross. I saw the feet of Jesus that walked everywhere to bring good news to broken people everywhere that needed to hear the Word of Truth that would liberate them, also being nailed to the cross. I could hear in my imagination the pounding of the nails into the wood of the cross. But by far, the worse part for me, the last straw, was when I saw the face of Jesus covered with human spit. I could not grasp what I was seeing. My tears began to pour out, flowing onto my cheeks, as the gospel reading continued. Jesus then continued to endure even more abuse at the foot of His cross – with soldiers mocking and jeering at Him, rolling dice to see who would win and get to keep His garments, and sadly, the absence of eleven of the twelve disciples that were His closest companions.

My boyfriend turned to me and said "what is the matter? You've heard this story before." I said "that's just it; it is not a story anymore. I feel like I *know* Him. Something is happening in me." It was different this time. I was no longer remembering a story about Jesus. I was *there*.

I looked up at Jesus on the cross and wanted to take Him down. But I sensed Him saying that He was dying for me so that I could be free. And I knew He was dying for every one of us, not just for me. And somehow, I knew that He was telling me this was the plan all along. He would die in my place so I could live eternally. He was not surprised by the cruelty of humans.

And, yes, I knew how the "story" would end. I knew about and believed in Jesus's resurrection – I knew that He rose from the dead on the third day, appeared to His disciples for 40 days, then ascended to heaven, seated at the right hand of His Father. I always believed that He was now alive, but beyond that, now I suddenly began to sense His presence close and personal, He was not only *alive*, but *alive in me* in a new way.

As is customary, at the end of service on the way out of the church all are invited to take a palm with us. When I randomly picked up my palm off the table in the back of the chapel, I have to say, it was a remarkably interesting palm - it was a single stalk that branched out into three palm leaves. I did not realize at the time how much that palm was a keen symbol of the Trinity. I brought it back to my apartment and draped it over my crucifix that hung on the wall over my bed.

For some reason after this experience at mass, I began having nightmares, spiritual in nature. I saw myself running in the dark outside trying to get from the campus to my apartment as I was being chased by an unknown "monster." In the dream I saw what I knew to be Mother Mary in the sky. She was urging me to run and was watching me. In the dream I began reciting what I now know to be a psalm – "the blood of the lamb upon my head will protect me from all evil." When I awoke, I felt a permeating sense of peace, and while I was making my bed, I looked up at the crucifix and saw that the tip of the stalk of my palm had turned red! I took it down, looked at it, and touched it. It was not wet or anything; however, it literally had red splatter marks on the side of the stalk. I put the palm back draped over the crucifix. Later in the week my roommate came into my room, and I showed it to her. She was stunned! It was unexplainable.

All during that Holy Week I kept getting a strong desire to pray and then I would get all choked up again like I did on Palm Sunday. Even when I turned on the TV and saw a commercial with a crippled child in a wheelchair, I would get tears again and just weep. I cried on and off for several days, as if someone I loved deeply had just died. On Wednesday of Holy Week, I prayed "Lord, I know you are real, I know you are here with me, I know that you rose from the dead. I love you so much, but I don't even know how to pray. I don't have the words to tell you how I feel."

Shortly after I spoke those words, I laid face down on my bed in my pillow, and I felt my sorrow change, instantly. I felt a deep warm feeling of peace inside, followed by a burst of joy bubbling up inside me. For some reason I began to speak aloud syllables that were unknown to me. It was a little bit like a giggle, except the syllables seemed to be more formed somehow, as if my emotions were free to speak in a newfound language. I later learned that this was the gift of tongues that I had received. I will share more about that later in this book, but for now, suffice it to say that the joy was as overwhelming as the sorrow had been, and I knew that I had found new depth in my relationship with the Lord. I wondered what was happening to me, so I got up from my bed and went over to the mirror over my bureau to see myself! In the mirror I saw that my face was glowing with happiness, and I watched my mouth moving, speaking a language that I did not know!

Later I would learn that the gift of tongues is a gift of prayer, and from my experience I learned firsthand that it was a gift of prayer, because I received the gift after I told God I wanted to pray but didn't have the words to tell Him how I feel.

Romans 8:26-27 says:

[26] In the same way, the Spirit helps us in our weakness. We do not know what we ought to pray for, but the Spirit himself intercedes for us through wordless groans. [27] And he who searches our hearts knows the mind of the Spirit, because the Spirit intercedes for God's people in accordance with the will of God.

I proceeded to go on about my day. I did have finals to prepare for. I did not dwell on the experience but enjoyed feeling peace and joy coursing through my veins at a level I never had experienced before. A few days later when I was walking to math class, I noticed what a beautiful spring day it was, and I loved seeing the bright yellow daffodils around me. The entire world seemed like it was in Technicolor! Not just from springtime, but from the joy that was still in my heart - it was still overflowing, like a bubbling brook. As I walked, I said aloud (Italians do that sort of thing…we talk to ourselves out loud): "What a beautiful day!" But instead of saying those words in English, I spoke in "that language!" It again felt as if my emotions could speak, and I simply let the syllables continue to flow out of me. I thought, "Oh no, this did not go away! I wonder what is happening to me! I should go and talk to the campus priest."

I made an appointment with the college priest, and he was very attentive and kind. I shared my experience, starting with the Gospel reading on Sunday, followed by my overwhelming grief and weeping, and desire to pray. Given it was towards the end of the semester, heading toward final exams, he asked me if perhaps I might be studying too hard! He thought I might have exhausted myself and possibly reverted to baby talk. However, even he was not satisfied with his own explanation, so he went on to recommend two books that I might find helpful – one was "A Cloud of Unknowing" and the other was "St. John of the Cross."

When looking back on that meeting with him, I always appreciate that he never doubted the authenticity of my experience, even though he could not explain it. All I knew was that I was changed, and I knew beyond all doubt that whatever had happened to me was real. Even though I could not explain it, I knew that God and I had connected and that I would never be the same again. Like the scene from the Wizard of Oz where Dorothy emerges from her house that had been tossed by a tornado and then abruptly landed in Oz, as in the movie where the film goes from black and white to color, I experienced my life also going from black and white to color. I began to notice that I was becoming more compassionate, more aware of others around me that were hurting, and more drawn to wanting to spend time with God. The closest way to describe it was that it felt like falling in love. I felt God's love for me, and I felt my love for God in return.

After that experience, which is often called "being filled with the Holy Spirit," I wandered, rather, glided, along in an afterglow-bubble of joy. "Fully alive" comes to mind. I wasn't even asking my typical questions such as "what happens next?" But I did wonder "what is this

29

that happened to me?" and "will it last?" I did not need anything more than this warm sense of the alive and exciting presence of God with me, yet it was still very much a mystery to me. I did not want to ever wake up from this beautiful dream, if that is what this was.

I said in the first paragraph that this experience defined the rest of my life, and that it was a turning point in my life. It was a turning point because there would be no turning back, or away from Jesus as Lord of my life. That does not mean that I would never have fears or doubts or make mistakes or bad choices for the rest of my life. That is not possible on this side of heaven, because sin will always be at work against us; but Jesus will always provide the way out of sin. Since this turning point, I can never deny the reality that Jesus is alive and present with me.

If these miraculous moments were not enough, here I am forty five years later, searching online to find a picture of the inside of Goddard chapel so I could include it in this chapter. In my search, I discovered pictures of the stained glass windows in the chapel that I never noticed before. In particular, take a look at the picture of the three windows that are on the left side of the chapel as you enter the chapel and walk down the aisle. The first window on the far left is a stained glass window of a palm branch!

Stained glass windows Goddard Chapel, Tufts University
(https://chaplaincy.tufts.edu)

What About Your Story?

We are all unique, and God knows and loves each of us intimately and personally. He finds unique ways of revealing Himself to each of us, so our experiences may be very different.

What is common to all of us, however, is that Jesus knocks on the door of our heart and invites us to respond to His love and let Him in (Revelation 3:20). Having what we think is a perfect life is not the requirement, opening the door to Him is.

Letting Jesus into your heart is the beginning of living a life of KNOWING that He is with you always. And there is a peace beyond understanding that comes with that.

No Jesus
No Peace.
Know Jesus
Know Peace.

Author Unknown

Finding Answers and Finding Community

One late morning, not long after I met with the chaplain about my experience, my eyes were directed to an 8.5 x 11 paper sign nailed to a tree trunk while I was walking along the Tufts campus. It simply read "Tufts Christian Fellowship prayer meeting 12:00 - 12:30 pm daily Monday-Friday in Goddard Chapel." I must have walked past that sign on that tree for almost 3 years, yet never noticed it. On this day it was as if the sign was flashing my name in neon lights, telling me about and beckoning me to become aware of this daily prayer meeting. It felt significant somehow, and the invitation kept gnawing at me. So, the next day I went to the prayer meeting. It was not until writing this entry that I made the connection that I was being led right back to Goddard Chapel - the place where I got my palm and encountered the Holy Spirit on Palm Sunday – for a further unfolding of this season in my life of redirection and miraculous moments.

The prayer group was a nice group of about a dozen people, from a variety of Christian denominations. We sat in a circle, and someone led the meeting. I did not know at the time that there was an established leadership team who took turns leading the group each day. The meeting began with a scripture reading and a brief reflection on it, and we were all invited to share any insights we might have. After this time of reflection, the meeting shifted to a time of intercessory prayer, where we prayed for special intentions for ourselves or for others. Anyone who wanted could speak aloud a prayer request; usually it was a prayer of intercession for someone who was sick, suffering or in need of finding God; or for ourselves; or for the obvious prayer during finals asking for help to get a good grade on an upcoming exam! Then we bowed our heads and closed our eyes and different people spontaneously prayed out loud for one of the requests that had been presented, as they were led to pray for (e.g., they would lead that particular prayer because they could either connect to the situation from their own personal history, or they felt a prompting to intercede about it) until all the requests were prayed for.

During this time of prayer, I opened my eyes and looked around the prayer circle, and saw that everyone's head was still bowed, with their eyes closed. I was in discovery mode, eagerly searching to learn more about where I had landed and even more about the people that were also at this meeting. Across the way from me was a woman I recognized as having lived in my dormitory my freshman year. I knew she was a Messianic Jew (a Jewish person that believes Jesus was the Messiah.) I could not help but notice that her lips were moving the same way that mine were when I had run to the mirror in my bedroom to observe myself when I first began speaking "that language!"

After the meeting I went up to her and I told her I saw her praying quietly to herself with her lips moving, and briefly shared my experience with her. I asked her if she could help me understand the new language, and especially if it was biblical! As it turned out, she was a senior now, and was one of the leaders of the Tufts Christian Fellowship. She opened her Bible and showed me in Acts of the Apostles in the New Testament where the gift of tongues was first experienced by the disciples on Pentecost, and then further gave me references from Paul's letters in the New Testament (especially 1 Corinthians 12.)

She also told me about a weekly prayer group she was attending, at a Catholic church no less, on Friday evenings, and suggested that I join her. She said I would fit in even more than she did because I was a Catholic. The church was located at the foot of the Tufts campus and was a short and easy walk. She said the Friday evening prayer group was called a "charismatic" prayer group. I asked what that meant, and she said "charism" is a word meaning "gift," and that they prayed using the "gifts of the Holy Spirit."

So, it was a Messianic Jewish woman who took me to my first Catholic Charismatic Prayer meeting where I learned about all the gifts of the Holy Spirit, including speaking in tongues. I was stunned and thought "Catholics know about this? This is the best kept secret in the Catholic Church!" I learned that not only was this move of the Holy Spirit happening in the Boston area, but that it was worldwide. Although the Pentecostal movement began in 1906 on Azusa Street in Los Angeles, California, the Charismatic Renewal first occurred in the Catholic Church in the United States at a retreat of college students at Duquesne University not long after Pope John the 23rd had prayed for a new Pentecost in the 1960's, then again at Notre Dame during a mass said on campus. The Lord was moving on the Catholic college campuses. From the campuses, there was a resurgence of the charismatic gifts spreading to the parishes, not only in the Catholic Church but in other Christian denominations as well, including the Messianic Jewish synagogues.

My experience taught me two fundamentally important things: the Holy Spirit desires unity among all Christian believers; and that finding God was not about *my holiness* but rather about *my love* for Jesus and an openness to being in relationship with Him. I was not living a holy life when I first had this experience on Palm Sunday, nor was I seeking such a life. Receiving a gift of the Holy Spirit is not a reward for being holy. It was not about my holiness, or worthiness; rather, it was about loving Jesus. And, I needed to receive the Holy Spirit in order to even *want* to begin a journey toward holiness.

Praying in tongues is a gift of prayer, and even though I could not understand the words I was uttering I learned that the Holy Spirit was praying through me, and that the prayer was perfect. I no longer needed to find the right words to pray, and I was able to even pray for people I did not know! For a perfectionist, that awareness was quite a relief, and was empowering. God taught me that the gifts of the Holy Spirit have a purpose – God's purpose. He equips us with gifts, gives us tools if you will, to continue the mission of Jesus to establish His kingdom here on earth as it is in heaven.

When I went home for Easter, saddled up with my newfound experience, knowledge, and absolute excitement, I eagerly blurted out "I speak in tongues!!!!" to my family at the dinner table. Needless to say, my father was quite upset and almost pulled me out of college thinking I had fallen into a terrible cult at college. My sister on the other hand wanted to know what had happened to me and she easily recognized my newfound joy and excitement. That night I slept in her room so we could do the sisterly "talk all night" thing. At this point I wasn't sure if I could pray in tongues at will, or even if it was ok to let anyone hear me speak in tongues out loud, so I said to her, let's just pray the "Our Father" prayer together, and if I feel that language coming, I will pray it out loud so you can hear it. Well, we held hands and prayed the Lord's Prayer together, and then I felt the tongues welling up within me, so I softly spoke the syllables out loud. My sister began to cry. She did not know why she was crying except that she knew it wasn't "me" praying, and that it was somehow really God near us.

35

That was the first time I prayed in tongues aloud with someone else with me. After the long Easter weekend, I returned to college for the remainder of the semester.

Weeks later she called me at school to tell me that she also received the gift of tongues. After I left to return to college, she had prayed, "Lord, if my sister has this, I want it too!" (a typical little sister prayer, right?) The Lord honored her prayer and her true desire to be closer to Him. Judy and I began a journey of praying, seeking, and learning together.

At the end of the spring semester, when it was time for me to go home for the summer, I expressed at the Friday night charismatic prayer meeting that I hated to miss being able to come each week. They told me that there was a directory of charismatic prayer groups all over the world and the following week, the leader obtained and gave me one. I looked up my state, hoping to find a prayer group in my area. To my surprise, there was a Catholic Charismatic prayer group in my hometown parish, where I grew up, about two miles from my parents' home! My sister, and her boyfriend Dan (who is now my brother-in-law) and I began attending the meeting every week. We were the youngest members of the group. Soon after, my parents started to attend because they were still so worried that now both of their daughters were in some kind of cult. On the first night that they went to it, God provided something special for them –the prayer group had a rare visitor, a Catholic priest, and he gave a teaching about the Charismatic Renewal at the meeting! My parents were not only comforted by the fact that a priest was there, but that he also took the time to talk with them afterword, reassuring them that this "movement" was legitimate, authentic, and accepted by the church. It is so precious to me the way the Lord used their love of their children to draw them into a closer relationship with Him and bring them into this experience of an intimate prayer group. We attended that prayer group as a family for about 20 years. My family was transformed (we each thought that the others were becoming nicer people) into a small community of spirit-filled believers!

In conclusion, I was twenty years old when I received the gift of tongues in the privacy of my college apartment bedroom. I thought my life would never be the same again! And it wasn't – my world really did go from black and white to color and has never gone back since that Palm Sunday. However, I mistakenly thought that my life would be free from struggles, pain and even my own sinful nature from that moment on. I mean, after having had such a powerful spiritual experience, how could anything bad ever happen again! Well, I would later learn that I still had my sinful nature and free will to contend with, as well as life's continual trials, because we are not yet in heaven, still exiles here on planet earth. However, there was one permanent significant difference now - I knew that I knew that I knew that God was with me, always, as His Word promises "I am with you always, even 'til the end of time." (Matthew 28:20). I also knew that I was no longer lost but found, because I knew that Jesus was the Way, and if I stayed close to Him, I would be on the right path.

We all must continue to live our lives here on planet Earth, and we are certainly not yet in heaven while we are here. I experienced many trials the following year that I could not have endured without the comfort and strength of the Holy Spirit in my life. I believe that God gave me His Holy Spirit at that time in my life because He knew what lay ahead, and that I would need Him to survive the difficulties that were coming my way.

I still have the three segments of the Palm draped over my cross in my bedroom. But I lost the miraculous stalk twenty-two years later (believe it or not, it was still red with the splatter marks) because I cut it off to get it analyzed. After all those years, and showing it to various people in my life, my stubborn engineering brain wanted to know what it was made of. I cut the stalk off from the branches, and as I was cutting it, I heard the voice in my mind whispering, "are you sure you want to do this?" I ignored the still, small voice, and gave my precious gift from the Lord to someone who was going to take it to a chemist for an analysis. After waiting a long time to find out the results, I finally asked about it and learned that he had forgotten all about it and lost it. The Lord simply did not allow it to be analyzed. The consequence of my curiosity is that I no longer have it to treasure and share with others. It is one of the biggest regrets of my life. Perhaps the stalk turned red, like leaves do in the fall, but that doesn't satisfy me because I have yet to ever see a palm do that, even in nature still on the tree.

That palm commemorated a miraculous moment in my life, and I miss being able to share it with the new people that have come into my life since then. There is nothing free about free will, as we pay the price for our free choices made when we ignore the "still, small voice."

Here is a picture of the chapel where I attended service on Palm Sunday, and the raised platform where the daily Tufts Christian Fellowship met.

Stained glass windows Goddard Chapel,
Tufts University (https://chaplaincy.tufts.edu)

What About Your Story?

Can you recall a time when you felt directly led by God, e.g., through: _may tries_

- an inspired thought, or _— may tries_
- a visible sign that you somehow noticed, as if it was calling out to you to be seen, or _yes._
- a sentence in a book you are reading, or _yes_
- a Scripture passage that suddenly breaks into your whirlwind of thoughts and redirects your thinking, or _yes_
- a word spoken by a friend, or a stranger, which seemed to settle upon you and provide some kind of answer or direction? _y_

Ask the Holy Spirit to open your spiritual eyes and ears to the next life-giving step in your journey.

The Blizzard of '78

Again, I would prefer to keep this account focused on what God did for me, rather than on the circumstances of my life at the time of these miraculous interventions, but I must provide you some context so you can appreciate what God did for me, and for the account to make sense. I will keep the background as brief as possible because it was a heart-wrenching time for me. I included the necessary details to be able to show how great was God's intervention, and how He saved me and my future.

After my spiritual conversion experience in my junior year of college, I was still in a relationship with my high-school boyfriend in our senior year. We had been going together for 5 years, and I was imagining what our future might look like. I was sure I was headed for an engagement ring after college graduation. However, in January 1978, the last semester of my senior year, the relationship was abruptly ended when I discovered at a dormitory party that he was (and had been) seeing someone else; the freshman girl who lived across the hall from me, no less. It was devastating to me emotionally...a complete shock that I needed time to believe, cope with, and try to keep the wheels of my stellar academic experience on track. Depression fell heavily upon me, and I started missing classes because I could not stop spontaneously weeping, nor could I get myself out of bed to attend them. After several weeks of this, the Lord sent me a beautiful Christian friend who came over one day and said "Susie, you have got to get up. You cannot throw it all away…" She would not leave until I got up, showered and got dressed, then she escorted me to see my senior advisor professor to help get me reengaged with my purpose of being at college, and a plan of action to graduate. My advisor was empathetic to my situation and suggested that I move to another dormitory, so I would not have to see the "new couple" every day. He said that he would speak to my other professors on my behalf, and we agreed that I would start going to all my classes again. I promised that I would, which for me was binding. I went through the motions and got myself up the next morning, but the thought of attending classes and studying was still beyond overwhelming. I prayed "Lord I need a time out; I just can't cope right now."

As I was praying, and grieving, I heard that still small voice within me that could not be denied, because it is somehow heard with the ears of our Spirit. I sensed the Lord saying, "you need to forgive her." Her? Are you kidding me? Forgiving her was not only something I did not want to hear, but it was also something I did not want to do, nor did I think I ever could do. Up until then I was so focused on forgiving my ex, that I didn't think too much about the freshman girl who lived across the hall, the one who used to come into my room first semester and feign interest in my future, asking me when I thought we would get engaged, etc. The Lord was guiding me to forgive *her*. As I wrestled with God about this, He reminded me that this was the greatest grace He gave us from the cross, when He said "Father, forgive them, they know not what they do." He somehow showed me that my healing was irrevocably inseparable from my choice to forgive her, and that forgiving her was meant to release ME from MY pain, so I could move on. Forgiving her was not in any way a statement that a betrayal had not been done to me.

41

I forced myself to get up from the floor (literally from the floor, because I had dropped to my knees asking God to take that directive away), then I walked to my door, opened it, walked what seemed to be a million mile walk across the hall, and knocked on her door. I think I was hoping she would not be in her room, so I was jarred when she opened the door. There we stood facing each other.

The most surprising thing for me was seeing fear on her face - I could not imagine anyone being afraid of me. Especially now, as I was so broken and powerless. What happened next was pure instinct. I reached out and hugged her and said "I forgive you. If things had been good between me and him, there would have been nothing you could have done to break us up." I do not know where those words came from, they just tumbled out of me. But those words were God speaking truth to me, as well as through me, and I learned from them. I then quickly turned around and went back to my room. God did not say that I had to stay and chat! They ended up getting married, and I don't think we ever came face to face again until I went to her husband's (my ex's) untimely funeral thirty-one years later, when he died at 52 years old from cancer. I told her I was sorry for her loss and that she had been a good wife.

To my surprise, after I forgave her that day in the dorm, I was indeed released from the gripping pain that had me paralyzed. I still had sorrow, but there is a certain joy that comes from knowing you just did something really right! Not only was I certain that I had scored some big points with the Lord, but a very tiny current of hope began to flow through me again, particularly about my future. But forgiving her, although a miracle all in its own, is not the moment I wanted to tell you about in this chapter. What followed this was the Blizzard of '78 on February 5, 1978.

This infamous blizzard caused one hundred fatalities, and 4500 people were injured. The entire state and other New England states were officially closed for an entire week. In my small world, all my classes were cancelled so I decided to find a way to get home to my family if possible. The trains were operating, but I had to walk through miles of deep snow to get to the nearest Amtrak train station to get home. I really wanted to be away from the drama in my dormitory, especially when all classes were cancelled, and people were just hanging out together in the dorms. I went home for a week and got some well needed love and rest. This was the first gift of some needed time out.

I returned to school with a new resolve and motivation to finish the semester successfully. I was back up to functioning mode again, and while I was walking to one of my engineering classes, I was hit by a car while crossing the street because I could not see over the very tall snowbank that was on the corner of a not very well plowed street. I was sideswiped and went down. I did not feel any pain, and my first thought was to reassure the assembling group of people around me, including the driver, that I was ok. My left arm sleeve on my leather coat was torn, and the impact was sufficient to damage the side mirror of the driver's car. My right thigh was numb, and I could not get up. I was in shock, but I did not want anyone to feel bad or worry about me. I ended up in the college infirmary.

This event caused my ex to go talk to the college dean because he was concerned that I might have deliberately thrown myself in front of the car! This resulted in me getting immediately moved out of my dorm, which of course was the most popular dorm on campus that everyone wants to be in, the one we had finally managed to get into senior year. I was moved to another dorm on the other side of campus (which was the least popular dorm on campus, hence rooms were still available), to get me away from having to constantly run into the new couple across the hall from my room. My friends and family helped me move to that infamous old dorm that still had open shared (we called them "gang") showers and the like! To be honest, I really did not care anymore at that point. I was as numb as my right thigh.

Fortunately, my engineering lab work was all completed before my last semester senior year. I do not think I would have been able to miss all those labs and make them up later. This second time-out resulting from being hit by a car on campus property allowed me a few more options for making up work than simply explaining to my professors about a painful break up would have granted me. Because of the accident I was able to make up exams that I had missed. Unfortunately, however, there was one professor that was never notified of my accident or situation - my Religion professor - because Religion apparently was not a course that the engineering curriculum thought much about! Ironically, this was the course I saved to take during my last semester senior year in order to enjoy it and finish off my four years with a little less stress – so much for that plan!

My religion professor had perceived me as "missing in action" and was not at all aware of all that had happened to me, and I was in danger of failing the course, which I did need as one of my electives to be able to graduate. So, the week before graduation I had to lay bare my life and share with him what happened to me to obtain permission to take the final exam late; by late I am talking about the actual week of graduation! I ended up getting a good grade on the exam, which had to be used to offset my low or missing grades on the other past assignments. I barely passed the course which should have been my most enjoyable and best class.

I received my Bachelor of Science Degree in Mechanical Engineering in May 1978 as planned, graduating Cum laude no less!

To be clear...I am not saying that the Lord caused a blizzard on February 5, 1978 for little ol' me, or the car accident. What I am saying is that the gift of time away from the pressure of completing my semester's work under such emotional duress was most definitely a miracle in my life.

From Jeremiah 29:11-14:

[11] "For I know the plans I have for you," declares the LORD, "plans to prosper you and not to harm you, plans to give you hope and a future. [12] Then you will call on me and come and pray to me, and I will listen to you. [13] You will seek me and find me when you seek me with all your heart. [14] I will be found by you," declares the LORD, "and will bring you back from captivity."

What About Your Story?

Can you identify a time in your life when you knew beyond all doubt that God had stepped in and rescued you from a destructive ending to a difficult circumstance? If so, how was it resolved? Were you at peace with the way things turned out?

Take a moment to give thanks to God for such times of His intervention either directly or through others who cared for you during your difficult time.

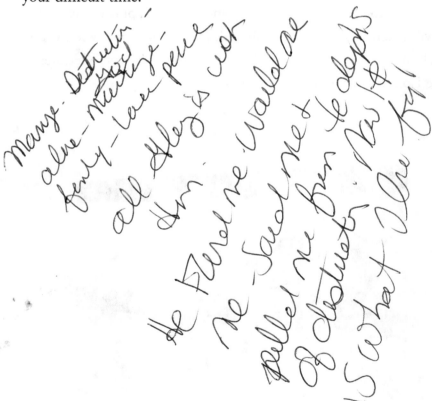

8

"Little Girl, Arise!"

After graduating college in May 1978, I began my first engineering career job in July 1978 at Pratt and Whitney Aircraft. I was still reeling from my senior year heartbreak and near misses, but I was hopeful to begin a new season of my life as a real engineer making a real salary! As a new-hire, I was not given much vacation time – you only got two weeks a year back then – which seemed like hardly a moment to a new college graduate.

I had a friend who was the son of Christian missionaries in Israel, and he was raised in Israel. His family was still serving there. During one conversation when he observed me sinking into my pit of self-pity, he said to me "when life gets tough, you can't just lie down and die!" Those words that he spoke to me have stayed with me, to the point that I can now catch myself being tempted to sink into that pit before I fully sink. When I sense my energy starting to drain, I pray and make a disciplined and deliberate choice not to lie down and give up. He extended an invitation to me to travel with him to Israel over the Christmas holiday (1978) and stay with his family, and that they would give me a personally guided tour of the Holy Land. Not only was that an incredible and beyond belief offer, but because the pending holidays were looming over me (the first Christmas without my ex) the thought of going away over Christmas seemed like a wonderful idea to me. Even more so, going to the Holy Land to see where Jesus walked was a dream come true. And because of my engineering job, I now had the funds to take such a trip.

It still blows my mind that my very first airplane trip was to Israel! It was quite a long flight, with one stop in Switzerland. I stayed with his family in a real home in Israel and it still is one of the most beautiful memories of my life. They graciously showed me the sites where Jesus walked, introduced me to freshly grown food from the region, prepared meals at home, and taught me a lot about the Arab side of the country as well as the historic holy places I longed to visit. It was a special time because I wasn't part of a guided tour, which allowed me to linger where I wanted to. I saw Ashkelon and palm trees and poinsettia trees near the Mediterranean, Bethlehem, Nazareth, Old and New Jerusalem, north to Mount Carmel, and then south to climb Masada, and saw the Dead Sea along the Jordan border which still had land mines. I was amazed that in a country about the size of Massachusetts, there were so many different climates! I experienced both snow and the Mediterranean climate in the north, and 80 degrees in the arid southern desert.

With all these sacred and beautiful sites, there was one strange "missing link" for me. I never got to visit and pray in the Garden of Gethsemane. I cannot recall why not; it must have been due to weather or time limitations. However, later during our trip he took me to Yad Vashem, which is the museum commemorating the unthinkable and terrible Holocaust. When the Jews that managed to escape their home country where they had lived and worked, or death in horrid concentration camps, upon arriving in Israel they would go to this place to register in hopes of reconnecting with other family members. Part of the missionary work my friend's parents did in Israel included helping drive survivors, many who were maimed from having been tortured, to a safe place where they could hope to be reunited with loved ones. It was heartbreaking. From the second I arrived at this museum I felt the spiritual heaviness and atrocity of what had happened. There were graphic photos, and items such as the shoes, teeth, gold fillings and other remnant signs of a life that had been cruelly stolen. I heard the Holy Spirit whisper "This is the Garden of Gethsemane." I just stood there in silence to let those words sink in. I realized that if I had gone to the Garden of Gethsemane with the beautiful gardens of palm trees, I would not have felt the gravity of the Lord's pain nearly as much as I did by being in this museum. So, I prayed with Jesus there, in the garden of Yad Vashem.

Taking that trip was also a big step out of my past and into my future. The Lord was inviting me out from dwelling on past hurts; you know the kind of thinking that focuses on what could have been, or what should have been. The Lord was inviting me out of the prison of unforgiveness that I was still locked in. I did not recognize it as unforgiveness, because I had said the words "I forgive" countless times over! I thought it was depression and despair, which is part of it, but more likely a by-product, not the root cause.

I do not know who the original author of the following statement was, but whoever it was, the Holy Spirit truly inspired that person. The quote is: "Unforgiveness is like drinking poison and hoping the other person dies." So, the person that stays sick, or broken, or stuck, is the person that will not forgive (and I might add, forget.) The Lord showed me that part of forgiving involves disciplining one's mind to stop dwelling on the old events, even if they truly were unjust and wrong. I realized that I was saying the words "I forgive," but I said them without intending to forget a thing! I did not want to forget a single word that had been spoken, nor a single word that should have been spoken. I began to learn that forgiving releases the person that was hurt from continually being hurt repeatedly by each memory of the old conversations and the old dreams. By forgetting I do not mean a complete denial or loss of memory, rather, forgetting in the sense of choosing to leave it behind and move on. That is when the memories became more like a movie that I have seen rather than an experience happening to me (again) today. I needed to be released from unforgiveness and living in the past in order to move forward into a future full of hope - the rest of my life - that the Lord was inviting me to step into.

So, this became a year of turning my eyes toward "the world out there." I realized that I wanted to travel, and I finally had the financial means to take some trips beyond gas money for my car. My dilemma was that I did not want to travel with other people, because I craved time alone with God, and for me vacation was a getaway for a quiet and peaceful time, and for prayer -- I was not a party animal-- yet I was afraid to travel alone. I wanted to be by myself to dream again, yet I wanted to be safe. I talked with some of my slightly older colleagues at work and one of them, my engineering mentor, suggested that I take a trip to Bermuda. He shared how beautiful the beaches were, and that I could fly there, get a cab that would take me right to a bed and breakfast (more affordable for a new college graduate) and I could easily and safely walk to a beach or restaurants. After toying with the idea, I woke up one morning saying, "I'm going to do this!" So, I booked a trip to Bermuda. The morning of the flight I panicked. I just could not imagine having the courage to fly alone, arrive alone, and relax for a week by myself! As only the Lord can do, He spoke a word to me "Little girl, Arise!" It was from one of my favorite Scripture passages from the Gospel of Mark 5:21-24, 35-43 where Jesus raises a girl back to life:

> [21] When Jesus had again crossed over by boat to the other side of the lake, a large crowd gathered around him while he was by the lake. [22] Then one of the synagogue leaders, named Jairus, came, and when he saw Jesus, he fell at his feet. [23] He pleaded earnestly with him, "My little daughter is dying. Please come and put your hands on her so that she will be healed and live." [24] So Jesus went with him.

> [35] While Jesus was still speaking, some people came from the

house of Jairus, the synagogue leader. "Your daughter is dead," they said. "Why bother the teacher anymore?"

³⁶ Overhearing what they said, Jesus told him, ~~"Don't be afraid; just believe."~~

³⁷ He did not let anyone follow him except Peter, James and John the brother of James. ³⁸ When they came to the home of the synagogue leader, Jesus saw a commotion, with people crying and wailing loudly. ³⁹ He went in and said to them, "Why all this commotion and wailing? The child is not dead but asleep." ⁴⁰ But they laughed at him.

After he put them all out, he took the child's father and mother and the disciples who were with him, and went in where the child was. ⁴¹ He took her by the hand and said to her, *"Talitha koum!"* (which means "Little girl, I say to you, get up!"). ⁴² Immediately the girl stood up and began to walk around (she was twelve years old). At this they were completely astonished. ⁴³ He gave strict orders not to let anyone know about this, and told them to give her something to eat."

I heard the word so clearly, as if it was shouted into my bedroom! And I felt the Lord's hand reach out to me, to help me out of my bed and take the next steps toward new life - in this case, the freedom to travel on my own knowing He would be there with me.

I made the trip, and I will never forget the cab ride from the airport to my bed and breakfast. I thought I was in paradise! I saw the turquoise color of the ocean, white and pink sand, and flowers everywhere! The scents were as beautiful as the views. And I did feel safe. It was breathtaking.

Here is where it got interesting (aka miraculous) ...

While riding in the cab to my bed and breakfast destination, I overheard another party talking about where they were staying and that there was going to be a prayer meeting on Friday night at someone's home that lived on the island. I remember thinking "there are some people that are actually lucky enough to live here?" As I listened (you could not help but listen we were in one bus-like vehicle), I introduced myself and said that I could not help but hear them and I asked what kind of prayer meeting they were going to. Can you guess the answer? A charismatic prayer meeting of course. Before they got to their hotel, they wrote the address on a piece of paper for me. Long story long, I took a cab to the address of the home and found myself at a beautiful prayer meeting with a music ministry that was just a baby grand piano in the home, and everyone singing praise and worship songs! I was familiar with some of them, but many were new to me, and they were so powerful! I wanted to write them down so I would not forget them. The one that really stuck in my mind was "Lord You are more Precious than Silver." It captured how I truly felt. Living with and now traveling with the Lord was quite the adventure! I brought the song back to my prayer group when I returned home.

They concluded the prayer meeting asking God for His continual protection from hurricanes, which was a new kind of prayer to me. Those fortunate enough to live on such a beautiful island as Bermuda did have to contend with the threat of the destruction of their homes, beaches and even lives, from one bad hurricane. After the meeting we had light refreshments and then a woman who lived near my bed and breakfast offered to drive me back to my place.

When we got to my place, we decided to join hands and pray for each other, as we most likely would never see each other again. When the charismatic renewal first began, we joined hands quite readily and prayed on the spot spontaneously. It was sad when we lost that initial fervor. So, my newfound friend and I joined hands and prayed in tongues for each other (the beauty of praying in tongues is you can intercede for someone without knowing a thing about them, or details about their need, trusting that the Holy Spirit is praying the perfect prayer through you.) After we prayed, I saw something very clearly. I had never had a vision before, and I am not sure that is what I had, but this is what I clearly saw: a little girl in a pretty dress, running out of a house onto a driveway waiting for the person who was arriving. When the car pulled in, a man got out and hardly even noticed the little girl. He just walked by her. I saw the grimace on her face.

Because my heart was beating rapidly (that often happens during a "God moment") I said to my friend "gee, I am picturing a little girl… etc.) She looked up at me and said that she had a difficult relationship with her father and that what I saw actually had happened to her and that it was a moment when she really believed she was not loved. Because the Holy Spirit chose to bring this memory to her through my "vision," we prayed specifically about it and that the love of God our Father would pour into that painful memory and heal it. She wept a mixture of old pain and new joy, especially because we both could not believe what God had just done! God wanted to set her free from fear of rejection, which was impacting her marriage and other relationships and had kept her bound.

I was reminded of what the Lord had whispered to me to help me get myself to the airport to take the trip. So, I decided to speak it to her in turn. I said to my new sister in the Lord:

"Little girl, Arise."

What About Your Story?

Can you recall a time that you were lifted by God, and made able to conquer something you were afraid of or dreading for a long time?

Ask Jesus to help you arise from whatever may be holding you back.

Receiving Inspired Teachings

To the extent possible, I have presented these chapters in the chronological order as they occurred in my life. This entry, however, is more of an evolution over time. As I continued seeking God in my prayer life, I became more aware of the Holy Spirit moving in my life. At one point, I sensed a new way that God seemed to be choosing to work through me. In hindsight, I believe that after receiving the gift of tongues, I was also given a gift of teaching, yet to be realized. It was easy to recognize the gift of tongues because it happened in an instantaneous moment; a moment where I went from not knowing about it, to suddenly being able to pray in a new language, at will. I have come to believe that the gift of tongues unlocked doors to other gifts of the Holy Spirit, which are meant to be tools in a Christian's toolbox, for the purpose of sharing the gospel of Jesus, and to help people grow in faith.

After I followed the Spirit's leading to the Tufts Christian fellowship, I had my first experience with what I am calling a gift of teaching. It started with a real thirst to read the Bible, and by read I do not mean reading the Bible cover to cover. Rather, I would pray for a few minutes, and then I would ask the Lord to teach me something through His Word, the Bible. I would then either randomly open to a page, or in much rarer moments, I would sense a specific chapter and verse in my mind, and I would then turn to it. When I randomly opened to a page, I would scan the two pages facing me, pray in tongues and wait. Invariably my eye would be drawn to a certain paragraph, as if it were in neon lights, much like the way I first saw the sign posted on the tree trunk for the daily prayer meeting in the Tufts chapel. This time in my life, when I was sensing and following the Lord's leading to specific prayer communities and prayerful people, reminded me so much of the childhood Treasure Hunt game we used to play at friends' birthday parties. The hosting parent(s) would give us a list of items to find, along with clues as to where the items were hidden. We were then sent out to walk in a designated neighborhood (pre-arranged by the hosting parent of the party) to find the items on the list. It was such an adventure and a thrill to find what we were searching for! And, so was the experience of "following God's breadcrumbs" along my path to find what He was leading me to.

One day while praying in my room and reading my Bible I turned to the final prayer of Jesus in John 17:20-23 when He prayed "My prayer is not for them alone. I pray also for those who will believe in me through their message, that all of them may be one, Father, just as you are in Me and I am in You,...so that they may be brought to complete unity." I was overwhelmed with the realization that Jesus prayed for ME at that time right before He was arrested in the Garden of Gethsemane, as well as for His disciples at that moment in history. Maybe this was commonly understood by many, but the way God revealed it to me was what I am calling "my miraculous moment," because Scripture was beginning to come alive for me. As the Word of God drew me in, I would also receive a new understanding of an even fuller message that I knew was meant to be shared. I felt that it was a "preach-able" message, and not a fleeting insight just for me to enjoy.

56

One day at the Tufts Christian daily noontime prayer meeting I got up the courage to volunteer to take a turn leading the prayer meeting, which mostly involved choosing a selected Scripture and giving a very brief teaching on it. I chose to use the reading I had received in my room from John 17. As I began to read it aloud to the group, I was surprised at the passion I felt when I read it aloud and I then proceeded to extrapolate on it. I shared how beautiful it was to me that Jesus was aware of us believers that would come so far in the future. We all took a moment to appreciate that Jesus had prayed for each of us, and that He knew us well before we ever knew Him. I also shared about the fulfillment of His prayer witnessed by our oneness at this very prayer meeting – here we all were, from a variety of different Christian denominations, gathered to pray for each other and for unity in the Body of Christ. It was a long while before I ever shared anything publicly like that again, but I never forgot the way it felt being "given the words" to speak. The experience of the Holy Spirit's gift of teaching was like praying in tongues; the language syllables or the message flowed effortlessly from my spirit right to and through my mouth, as opposed to coming from my brain. I do not mean to imply that thinking is not important, or not at all part of this process, but I experienced times when the Holy Spirit chose to speak directly through my voice, bypassing my critique or thoughts about pre-screening! How I wish the Spirit would always take over my mouth!

There is a remarkable account in the Old Testament, the Book of Numbers, about a man named Balaam who had a donkey, and God spoke words to Balaam through the donkey when he just wasn't getting it! Because it is so interesting, I will include it here so that you can easily read it because it is worth reading! It shows that God can work through any instrument, even a donkey, to make His Word known.

57

Numbers 22:21-39 Balaam's Donkey

²¹ Balaam got up in the morning, saddled his donkey and went with the Moabite officials. ²² But God was very angry when he went, and the angel of the Lord stood in the road to oppose him. Balaam was riding on his donkey, and his two servants were with him. ²³ When the donkey saw the angel of the Lord standing in the road with a drawn sword in his hand, it turned off the road into a field. Balaam beat it to get it back on the road.

²⁴ Then the angel of the Lord stood in a narrow path through the vineyards, with walls on both sides. ²⁵ When the donkey saw the angel of the Lord, it pressed close to the wall, crushing Balaam's foot against it. So he beat the donkey again.

²⁶ Then the angel of the Lord moved on ahead and stood in a narrow place where there was no room to turn, either to the right or to the left. ²⁷ When the donkey saw the angel of the Lord, it lay down under Balaam, and he was angry and beat it with his staff.

²⁸ Then the Lord opened the donkey's mouth, and it said to Balaam, "What have I done to you to make you beat me these three times?"

²⁹ Balaam answered the donkey, "You have made a fool of me! If only I had a sword in my hand, I would kill you right now."

³⁰ The donkey said to Balaam, "Am I not your own donkey, which you have always ridden, to this day? Have I been in the habit of doing this to you?"

"No," he said.

^{31} Then the LORD opened Balaam's eyes, and he saw the angel of the LORD standing in the road with his sword drawn. So he bowed low and fell facedown.

^{32} The angel of the LORD asked him, "Why have you beaten your donkey these three times? I have come here to oppose you because your path is a reckless one before me. ^{33} The donkey saw me and turned away from me these three times. If it had not turned away, I would certainly have killed you by now, but I would have spared it."

A few years later, after I had been attending the charismatic prayer meetings in my hometown, I began to feel myself gravitate toward certain readings, or to snippets from sermons or books, and even secular talks that I heard. I would jot them down. I began to see a pattern: I was gathering pieces together, still unsure of the purpose. Later I would discover that all the pieces fit together into a concise teaching with a clear theme tying them together. One such time I went to the head of the teaching ministry and said, "I think the Lord wants us to have a teaching about community." My intention was to tell her what I was "getting in prayer" and if she agreed, she could then assign the topic to one of the teachers on the teaching ministry to prepare and deliver it.

Prayer group teachings were usually about 15-20 minutes long. She looked at me for a long moment and then said, "I think that the Lord wants YOU to give that teaching because He is putting it on YOUR heart." I felt my anxiety rising; I never intended to appoint myself as a teacher. That is how I entered the teaching ministry in the Catholic Charismatic Renewal.

I was trembling when I stood up to deliver the message, my heart was pounding, I was sweating, and I honestly did not think I could get through it. After a shaky first few sentences, the words began to flow out of me, and I could feel my voice get stronger as I continued. At one point I even put down my notes and started to speak from my heart. It felt very much like speaking in tongues, only it came out in English! I was amazed how the Holy Spirit "kicked in" after I stammered out the first paragraph on my own.

After giving that teaching, people came up to me affirming the message. It intrigued me that each person was inspired by a different part of the talk, and some even quoted things that they heard me say that I did not even remember saying; it seemed that people each received a personal message from God that they most needed to hear at that time in their lives. I was amazed at how the infinite God could speak so uniquely to those who were seeking Him, using the same words.

This new gift matured in me to the point that I received invitations to speak at several large regional prayer meetings and retreats. I led Life in the Spirit Seminars which resulted in leading monthly Evenings of Refreshing at my parish for several years. As monthly teachings would come to me, and I jotted them down, these teachings were the scraps that I eventually compiled into my first published book "Scraps from the Father's Banquet Table: Spiritual Food for Thought."

Another miracle for me was to see how the Lord would first teach me something, over several weeks, and then at some later date, I would be invited to speak on that very topic, or on a topic of my choosing. The receiving of His message preceded the invitation I received to give a message.

That first invitation to read a Scripture verse aloud and expound on it to the Tufts prayer meeting opened a new door in my spiritual journey that resulted in years of future invitations to speak at retreats or prayer gatherings. After almost forty years, at this later time in my life, opportunities to speak dwindled, and even my physical voice has weakened to the point that I now need a microphone in order for people to be able to hear me well. I saw that instead of public speaking, my teaching gift has changed into a desire to write, but it is the same Spirit working in a different way to bring God's Word to people that want to hear the gospel preached through the instrument of God's choosing, whether it be me, or a donkey of His choosing.

Keeps us humble!

What About Your Story?

Have you found that you have a gift that God has uniquely given to you that is meant to be used to help others, as well as yourself?

God often uses other people to help us identify our gifts; for example, someone may tell you that something that you said, or did, made a real difference in their life.

Or that you have a special way of making them laugh, or open up, or comfort them when they are upset.

Recall the words from the movie "Chariots of Fire," when Eric Little said, "When I run, I feel His pleasure." When we are using our God-given gift, there is a sense of purpose, joy, and freedom coursing through us.

Ask the Holy Spirit to help you discover and release your gifts, and for the courage to step out and use those gifts to help others.

1 Corinthians 12:4–11 says:

"There are different kinds of gifts, but the same Spirit distributes them. There are different kinds of service, but the same Lord. There are different kinds of working, but in all of them and in everyone it is the same God at work. Now to each one the manifestation of the Spirit is given for the common good. To one there is given through the Spirit a message of wisdom, to another a message of knowledge by means of the same Spirit, to another faith by the same Spirit, to another gifts of healing by that one Spirit, to another miraculous powers, to another prophecy, to another distinguishing between spirits, to another speaking in different kinds of tongues, and to still another the interpretation of tongues. All these are the work of one and the same Spirit, and he distributes them to each one, just as he determines."

Staying "In" on the Town

After being part of my hometown church's prayer group for several years, and after becoming an official teacher in the group's teaching ministry, the leader of the group approached me about attending a two-week conference taught by some of the renowned leaders in the Catholic Charismatic Renewal in the 1980s. She thought this training would enhance my teaching gift in scripture and wanted me to have the opportunity to learn from these teachers. The conference was sponsored by the Catholic Charismatic Bible Institute at St. Mary's University in San Antonio, Texas in the summer of 1980. The keynote teachers were Father Brennan Manning, Father Richard Rohr, and Father George Montague, and another priest, Father Paul (I cannot recall his last name).

I arrived at the campus on a Friday afternoon, and the conference was to begin on Monday. I had planned to register, check into my room (we were staying in the college dormitories for this conference) and familiarize myself with the lay of the land. I could not wait to go into town and visit San Antonio to do some sightseeing and enjoy some awesome Mexican food!

Upon registering for the conference, I was told that Father Brennan Manning had offered to give a special, additional workshop on Saturday (the next day) entitled "The Heart of the Father." It was free, and people were raving about Fr. Manning's teachings. Not realizing the gift that was being offered here, I felt immediately disappointed, and a tug of guilt because I wanted to play in San Antonio on Saturday! My young 24-year-old mind thought that two weeks of teachings by four different priest-teachers was certainly going to enough - sufficient to refine my newfound teaching gift - not to mention the fact that I was worried that I would need some downtime to not get too overloaded. And did I mention how much I really wanted to see the town, including the aspect of spending some time outdoors?

Hearing other people speak with delight that this opportunity for an additional Saturday workshop with Fr. Brennan Manning was being offered, and the fact that I would still have the weekend in between the two weeks of classes free, I reluctantly signed up to attend. I do not know if it was peer pressure, or a case of the "shoulds and ought's," but somehow the Lord used all these things to get me there, including a Texas heat wave of 107 degrees! It is pretty funny when people say "oh, but it's a *dry* heat." Let me just say for the record, it felt all of 107 degrees and was ridiculously hot for this Connecticut girl!!

So, at 9:00 am on Saturday morning I found myself entering the air-conditioned auditorium for the workshop, and I took my seat about five rows from the stage so I could see and hear well. Fr. Manning began the day by saying this was going to be a workshop about the "Love of the Father." My heart sank...I thought I was going to learn about something new! I already knew (or so I thought) that Father God loved me - I mean He loves everybody! I was really struggling about whether or not to stay there for the entire day and give up my precious Saturday.

About 20 minutes into his first talk, I began weeping uncontrollably. I cannot even tell you why. Yes, I knew that God loved me, but I never ever realized how much. Nor did I realize how intimate His love was for me. I knew enough about the Holy Spirit to recognize that weeping was a sign of healing; that God was somehow moving in me and for me, to heal me of things I was not even aware of that needed healing. Healing is a lifelong process, but when the tears come, they come like a flood of release of pain, or else like a flood of release of joy. My weeping was so obvious that people I did not know were coming up to me and gently laying their hand on my shoulder to pray over me and comfort me. I just had never heard such words before that Fr. Manning was speaking! I think these people must have mistakenly thought that I had been abused as a child and was receiving a healing. Well, emotionally, from early formative years, I was carrying around wounds that I had yet to be able to realize or name.

Here are some quotes from Father Manning's workshop that day that are still emblazoned on my heart and memory:

"Do you know that God expects more failure from you than you do from your own self?"

"Do you know that it would be easier for you to contain the Gulf of Mexico in a teacup rather than for you to contain the wild and unconditional love of God for you?"

"Do you know that God loves you as you are, not as you should be, because none of us is the way we should be, or the way we think we should be?"

Those were the words that exploded within me because I realized that I was a perfectionist. As a student I strived to earn A pluses, trying to get the bonus questions right on the test. I thrived on seeing my parents' joy because of my good grades. For me, good grades meant I had earned my right to be loved and valued. It is not that my parents treated me that way, but for some reason, that is what I had come to believe. So, to hear that God expected more failure from me than I did from my own self just broke me. He loves me even when I fail.

Father Manning went on to say that most of us here have likely come to believe that Jesus is "God-like," but do we realize that God is "Jesus-like"? What a question! So, the God who sits on the throne watching me and keeping score…you mean to tell me He is really like Jesus, who hugged the adulterous woman, and heals people?

Then he quoted the passage from the Gospel of Matthew where Jesus said, "Whatever you did for the least of these, you did unto Me." (Matthew 25:40), and he asked us "what if you were to discover that the least of these, the very least of these that needed your love the most, was yourself? Would you do for yourself what you would do for someone else?"

He also taught us a simple but powerful prayer: "Father, I belong to you." When incorporated with your breathing (Father on the inhale, I belong to you on the exhale) this prayer brings a deep sense of being loved and peace.

I cannot put into words the impact this one day of teaching had on my heart and on my life. I met Jesus's Father, My Father, Our Father, in a new and personal way that day. The fact that I can quote Fr. Manning so precisely 40 years later is amazing to me. His words were burned into my heart, never to be forgotten. My teaching gift, as well as my prayer life, was empowered by my newfound freedom and relationship with Father God. I understood why everyone was so excited that Fr. Manning had agreed to do a Saturday workshop in addition to his one week of teaching. I was so glad I still had one more week to hear him teach.

I used to feel God's Love when I was "being good," "getting it right" by my own standard of measure, and then feel fear or shame when I wasn't having such a good day. I learned from Fr. Manning that God does not love that way. God's love is relentless, tender, eternal, infinite, unconditional, forgiving, and always searching for me and there for me. That kind of love makes me want to be my best self in return.

Besides the beginning of my healing of perfectionism, the real miracle was how God found the way to get me to give up my own tourist plans for the day and go to the workshop instead, and I went to San Antonio the following weekend. In fact, it was even better that following weekend, because after a week of being with other people at the conference, I had made some new friends, and they had some great ideas for sightseeing and restaurants that I did not even know about. We went "out on the town" together!

What About Your Story?

Has God ever nudged you to the point that you changed your plans mid-stream?

If so, how did it turn out?

Are you open to allowing God to change your plans? When God seems to take something away it is because He has something better.

Give God permission to work in your life, even if it means letting go of being in the driver's seat.

Divine Reset February '83

I could write an entire book on the events of this one month and the impact it had on my life. There were miracles entwined with miracles that healed my past, changed my present and prepared my future. The intricacies of God's plan still astound me. Of all the months in my life, February 1983 was the most complex, and the hand of God was brilliantly orchestrating a divine reset in my life.

After the events of January 1978 during my college senior year, and prior to February 1983, I leaned heavily on the Lord, asking the Holy Spirit to continue to help me forgive and move on. I was comforted often by my mentor and friend, Berthe Gagne, from our prayer group. She was its founder, and it began around her kitchen table with less than half a dozen women. She invited me to her home where she prayed with people, and in time she made me dinner as well. One night while going over the same issues, she told me about a priest, Father William Dudack, who offered pastoral counseling free of charge (that was a miracle in and of itself.) I contacted him, telling him that Berthe referred me, and he took me on as a client. I continued meeting with him for several years. I dedicated this book to Berthe and Fr. Dudack.

One day early in February 1983 I was sitting at my desk at Combustion Engineering, and I leaned my head on my hand as I was reading an extremely detailed technical specification and I needed a bit of a lift and physical support for my brain! While resting the side of my face on my hand, I felt a hard lump under my ear and above my neck, about the size of a walnut. I kept checking it and it did not move or collapse, and I wondered how long it might have been there and what it could be.

I decided to get up and take a walk within our multi-building complex. I felt "directed" to walk along a certain path from building to building, until I came to a set of lavatories three buildings away from my desk. I decided to stop in the lavatory, then turn around and head back to my desk. As I walked in the return direction, a pleasant looking handsome man was approaching and about to walk past me. We both broke out with a big smile, almost a chuckle, looked at each other, nodded hello and then both kept walking in our opposite directions. For some reason, I turned to do a double take and look back, and to my embarrassment and delight, so did he! It was quite spontaneous, and we both laughed again, and kept going our separate ways. (Nine years later we got married, but much had to happen in both of our lives before that was to be). Getting back to February 1983…

As I returned to my desk, I noticed there was a yellow post-it-note sitting on the floor that had apparently fallen off of someone's paper. I picked it up and it read "Bill - Susan Ceraldi (my maiden name) has 3 interviews on Friday in Nuclear Safety Engineering." My manager's name was Bill, so I thought it must be for him. I knew NOTHING of this or what it could be about. I was working in the proposal group in Fossil Engineering (designing coal, oil and gas fired units, not nuclear plants). This post-it note took center stage, and for the next moments, I forgot about the hard lump under my ear and the smile from an unknown handsome man and went in to see my manager with the note. He blushed profusely when I handed it to him. He invited me to sit down and then explained to me that I was on the list to be laid off due to a necessary staff reduction (I was the last one hired into the group), but he and Human Resources were trying to find a place for me in Nuclear Engineering where that branch of our company was hiring. It did not occur to me until much later that if I needed any medical care due to this lump under my ear, I was at risk of losing my health insurance. This day was surely THE whirlwind day of this whirlwind month.

After work, I went to a walk-in as my concern about the lump was mounting. After the doctor examined me, he called in other doctors to come in and examine me. That was unsettling because they seemed very serious and quite concerned. I finally asked, "what is it?" And they said that I needed to see an ear, nose, and throat specialist right away. They made an appointment for me for the next day, and I saw Dr. Russel Robertson at Hartford Hospital. He sent me for a test where they injected radioactive dye into my parotid gland. Sure enough I had a tumor the size of an almond in my parotid gland. I was immediately scheduled for surgery a week later, on February 22, which happened to be my mother's birthday. No one could tell me if the tumor was benign or malignant, or what the follow-on scenario might be like in either case.

I had begun dating someone I met at a restaurant – he was my waiter. That is a story for that awfully long book that I will never write called "My Mistake Moments." But for the sake of this account, suffice it to say that he broke up with me when he learned I had a tumor, before even learning whether it was benign or not.

I had to be admitted to the hospital the day before the surgery for preparation. The scary part for me as a single 27-year-old was not just having surgery, or even not knowing if the tumor was benign or malignant, but rather the fact that I had since learned that if it was malignant there was a chance I would wake up to a very disfigured face. Even if the tumor was benign, there was a risk of facial paralysis because there are so many facial nerves that go through the parotid gland. I was not afraid to die, I was afraid to have to live with half a face. Vanity oh vanity...my biggest fear was how I would look after the surgery.

The day before while I was awaiting surgery, there was a shift change of the nurses and my new nurse came in. What a surprise that was because it turned out that she was a friend from my high school graduating class! Her father was a deacon in the church I grew up in where our prayer group met. Not only did she know me, but she also knew my ex high school/college sweetheart, and she knew about our breakup (everyone seemed to...)

After briefly chatting about my upcoming surgery, she said "you know, [ex-boyfriend's] father is in a room down the hall recuperating from surgery. I could not believe my ears! I hadn't seen him in years and had liked him very much. She said I could visit him and encourage him to get up and take a walk with me. So, I was able to walk the hallway with him before my surgery. It was a very special moment for me - a chance to say goodbye to someone that had been important in my life, like family. I was amazed the Lord had timed both our surgeries this way.

Beyond that, my nurse also told my ex's mother when she was visiting her husband that I was five rooms down the hall awaiting surgery. She came to see me and was concerned for me. We enjoyed a hug and another goodbye to someone special in my life. To complete the Lord's plan, my ex came to visit his father that evening, and his parents told him about me, so he also came to see me. This became a moment where I felt that we had finally made peace with each other. He wished me well, and another goodbye. At this point I really started to think that I was going to die because the Lord had arranged such strange rendezvous!

Early the next morning Father Dudack came in to bless me before my surgery, and he arrived shortly after I had just been given my pre-surgery dose of a tranquilizer. I was groggy but when he came in, I recognized him, and I blurted out "Hi Father Dudack! I just saw [ex-boyfriend]! He came to see me!" Well, of course dear Father Dudack thought I was dreaming, hallucinating to be exact, and he told me to just try and rest. I kept saying "but it's true! It really happened!" and he gently put his hand on my face, blessed me, then left. Even in my tranquil state I was giggling on the inside because I knew how it must have seemed to him, and I looked forward to my next appointment with him, when I would tell him all that God had done. It was bizarre actually!

After my doctor asked me to sign my permission for surgery, I begged him to promise me that if the tumor was malignant and some of my face would have to be removed, that he would close me up first, and then wake me up before disfiguring my face, so I could prepare myself and even more, decide what options I might possibly have and what to do if that should happen. He gave me a weak nod yes, but it was not very assuring that he would keep such a promise if he felt he had to do something else.

My surgery took five hours and praise God the tumor was benign. The surgery was delicate because of the facial nerves. My surgeon Dr. Robertson was even able to leave part of my gland in my face, so I still have partial salivary function, as well as some protection for my facial nerves from the chilly air on my cheek in the wintertime. That is a story, too, because the partial saliva gland fused itself with my cheek's sweat glands when healing, so now, whenever I eat, my cheek sweats and I have to wipe it. That's ok, I'll take it! Happy to have a face to wipe!

In parallel to all these events, in February 1983 my beloved Uncle Bill who lived next door to me my entire life died of colon cancer that had metastasized to his liver and stomach. He fought it for a few years and was in the hospital when I was admitted for my surgery. My mother and I visited him on the day that I was admitted. I kissed him and he wished me luck and said, "I hope to God it is benign." After I was discharged from the hospital, my mother and I stopped in to see him, to say our final goodbyes as it turned out. I told him that my tumor was benign, and he whispered, "Thank God." I kissed him goodbye for the last time. He died a few days later. I was asked to do a reading at his funeral, which I was honored to do, and I did it with a massive bandage on my face. I was unable to pronounce "P's or B's" or put my lips together due to temporary facial paralysis from the surgery that thankfully eventually healed, but that did not seem to affect the reading.

During my recuperation time after my parotidectomy and grieving period, I read a book called "Prayerways: For Those that Feel Discouraged or Distraught, Frightened or Frustrated, Angry or Anxious, Powerless or Purposeless, Over-Extended or Underappreciated, Burned Out or Just Plain Worn Out", by Louis M. Savary. The book not only lifted me out of my slump, but also provided the next step in this time of God's divine reset of my life. While reading the book I learned that the author would be teaching a course on the book over a weekend at St. Joseph College in West Hartford, CT (I lived in Hartford), so I registered to take the class. Long story short I took that class, and then others, and realized I was not that far away from having enough courses to complete a master's degree program in Pastoral Ministry. I applied and was accepted into the program and graduated in 1985 with a Master of Arts degree in Pastoral Ministry and a Certificate in Spirituality. I did this over a two-year period, paying for this education with my engineering day-job salary and using my precious vacation time to attend classes evenings, Saturdays and in the summer. The curriculum was made up of counseling, spiritual direction, liturgy, and ministry courses. It was designed to train those who wanted to serve in the Church as lay ministers. I especially loved the incorporating a person's faith into the counseling healing process. Much healing can happen with such integration. After graduation, I was hired as a Crisis Counselor that addressed faith issues on the staff at Associated Counseling Professionals in Hartford CT. I had the privilege of collaborating with psychologists, psychiatrists, substance abuse counselors and marriage therapists. Together we were able to help many clients. I worked there one or two evenings a week for about 10 years before the director retired and closed the office. This was in addition to my full-time engineering job which paid my rent without me having to take on a roommate.

Speaking of my engineering job...shortly before my surgery I learned that one of the three job interviews I had in the nuclear engineering department panned out and I had a job offer, so I started a new job three weeks after my surgery. The Lord's timing was perfect (although He took me right to the edge...). And guess what else! My new job was in the exact area where I had taken what I thought was a random walk that day when I first felt my tumor and passed that handsome man in the hallway! I had never known or met those people before, or been in that building, or knew anything about the nuclear division of my company for that matter.

And yes, that handsome man that I had passed in the hallway the day I took my "random walk" sat not too far from my new boss, although I didn't realize that at the time because we did not officially meet until years later, and somehow never crossed paths. The Lord was preparing both of us for that future miracle of our marriage that would happen in His time, not ours. Years later we would officially meet when I was applying for a different job and went on the job interview. Because I never knew his name (and he did not know mine), I did not realize whose group I would be interviewing for, so it was quite a surprise for both of us when I showed up for my job interview. I thought to myself, "Oh my goodness, it's that handsome man in the hallway!" Given the professional context of our first official meeting, we went on to enjoy a professional working relationship for about six years. I am sad to say that during these six years, shortly after I started this new job, I met and went on to marry the man that would become my future abusive ex-husband. It was almost seven years before circumstances were such that Bob and I were both free to begin a courtship.

I would later learn that Bob had an episode of Bell's palsy around the same timeframe of my tumor, causing half the side of his face to be temporarily paralyzed on the same side of his face as my tumor. Could it be that he was interceding for me in that spiritual place that transcends our consciousness and time? Some of God's fingerprints are only discovered in hindsight.

Still more happened this month during my recuperation period. I was selected by a deacon in the Archdiocese of Hartford to represent our Archdiocese to help plan a New England Charismatic Conference at the Civic Center in Providence, RI. It was such an honor to have been chosen for this, and it required driving to Providence every other weekend starting in March 1983 until the conference in the summer of 1984. During that year and a half, I got to meet other leaders in the Charismatic Renewal from Vermont, New Hampshire, Massachusetts, Rhode Island, and Connecticut. We would meet for a few hours to discern the theme of the conference, the speaker for each talk, the music ministry, and other conference logistics. Ironically, the weekend that the conference was to be held, based on the availability of the Civic Center, ended up being August 3-5 in 1984. This was such a joy for me because August 3rd is my birthday! So, on the opening night of the conference weekend, 15,000 attendees sang happy birthday to me.

When I consider all that happened that month, and all that *had* to happen for these pieces of my life and self to come together, I am in awe of the infinite wisdom and power of God.

Our God is astoundingly perfect!

From 1 Corinthians 2:9-10:

However, as it is written:
"What no eye has seen,
    what no ear has heard,
and what no human mind has conceived"-
    the things God has prepared for those who love him -these
are the things God has revealed to us by his Spirit."

What About Your Story?

Was there ever a point in your life when you sensed a reset, as if you were taken out of one set of circumstances and placed into another?

If so, was it a change for the better?

If not, do you feel a need for a divine reset now? If so, ask God to lead you to the place that will be life-giving for you.

God Sees Differently than We See

This entry is about my miraculous experience while attending a Father Ralph DiOrio healing service in Worcester, MA in 1985. Father Ralph DiOrio is a Catholic priest renowned for having the charismatic gift of healing. He offered continuous healing services during the height of the Charismatic Renewal in the 1970s, 1980s and 1990s. He was the Director of Apostolate of Healing and was often called "The Healing Priest."

In addition to having the gift of healing, Father DiOrio also was given the charismatic gift called "Word of Knowledge." This is when the Holy Spirit imparts a supernatural knowledge to the recipient stating what God is doing. At a healing service Father DiOrio would begin by praying, with piano music softly playing in the background. He would then proceed to speak the thoughts that he was hearing in his mind, such as: "There is a woman here in a yellow sweater that has a hearing problem in her left ear...the Lord is healing you. There is a man who has been suffering from lung cancer...the Lord is removing the tumor. Go to your doctor and confirm it is gone." It was remarkable to be there in person and witness people standing up to receive the healings that he was calling out, or seeing people leave their crutches or wheelchairs behind. People often knew they were being healed because as Father DiOrio would call out a variety of specific illnesses in a row, without specifying individuals, they would feel warmth in the part of their body that was being healed. For example, he would name a series of diseases and say "the Lord is healing these illnesses now. Please stand up if you are receiving a healing." Then he would call people to come up to the microphone and testify to the healing they knew they had just received.

My reason for going to this service was to bring my cousin who has retinitis pigmentosa (RP). His mother and her sister (my father's two sisters) wanted to attend a healing service with my cousin in hopes he would be healed of this disease. At the time we went, he was not yet completely blind but there was no hope for a cure. My aunts heard about a bus trip going to one of Father's Worcester, MA services, and they asked me to go with them because they knew that I was very involved in the Catholic Charismatic Renewal.

I had been to one of Father's healing services a few years prior in 1981 when I took five of my confirmation class students to see him. I wanted them to be aware of such ministries in the church, and to see the Holy Spirit in action! That day turned out to be amazing because one of the young men that attended had a sports injury in his knee. When we got to the church I explicitly told my class to stay with me, that we needed to stay together so no one would get lost. I was feeling my responsibility as both teacher and chaperone. I wanted to be there to help them understand what they were experiencing as well as to bring them safely home to their parents who were already intrigued by such a field trip. As middle school teenagers would do, as soon as we entered the auditorium, the girls stayed with me as discussed, but the boys took off. I was livid! But at that point I simply prayed "Lord, please keep us all safe!"

At one point during the service Father DiOrio called out a healing, saying "there is a young man here with a knee injury. The Lord is healing your knee." The girls and I looked all around hoping to see our classmate stand up, but my student did not stand up to receive the healing. On the two-hour ride home he was very quiet, and the girls asked him "How is your knee? Was that knee healing for you?" He quietly answered, "I think so." He said he felt tremendous heat around his knee when Father DiOrio called it out. The girls asked him why he did not stand up when Father DiOrio called out the healing and he said he was too skeptical and afraid to believe it really was for him. I told him to thank the Lord and to claim the healing in the privacy of his own prayer time. I was amazed that God chose to give him a sign as that student was the most skeptical of the bunch.

So, in 1985 my cousin, aunts and I made the bus trip. We found enough seats to sit together not too far from the front of the auditorium. Early in the service, Father DiOrio called out several times that his piano player was sick and could not be there. He kept expressing how much he was missing the gift of that ministry, saying that it helped him to enter deeply into prayer and to release the healing and word of knowledge gifts that He had been given. Several times he repeated "The Lord is saying that there is someone out there that can play the piano and the Lord is asking you to come up and play." I could not deny the incredible heat that I was feeling coursing through me, and my heart started beating rapidly.

A flood of memories rushed in all at once, the first one being from kindergarten. There was a piano in our classroom and my teacher would play it and occasionally our teacher would invite anyone who wanted to play to come up and sit beside her on the piano bench, and "help her" play the song. I was so enthralled by her, Miss Rankin, and her ability to play the piano that I raised my hand right away and she called me forward. My part was simple – I had to hit the same note over and over on cue. I was supposed to be the bell in the song. I came to love the piano and went home excitedly saying to my parents "I played the piano at school today!" which soon morphed into "I know how to play the piano now!" I kept asking my parents for a piano and to take piano lessons. They did not have a lot of money but because of my persistence and enthusiasm, they managed to locate and buy an old used upright piano. They had to put it in our basement because there was no room in the house for it! When they saw me trying to play this piano, and my love for it, they researched and found a piano teacher that lived down the street from us. She came to our house to give me lessons, and I took lessons from when I was five years old until I was twelve.

My piano teacher did not belong to any studio, nor did she sponsor any recitals, so I never had to play in front of an audience. I began to have a bit of a stigma about that, starting to believe a lie that I wasn't a real pianist because I didn't have recitals like other piano students had. My teacher's style was more "honky-tonk." After those years of taking lessons, I continued to play on my own, in a much less structured manner, because I discovered that I could play by ear, i.e., if I could hum the song, I could play it. I was not drawn to the formality of classical music; however, in high school, at a talent show, I heard one of my classmates play a Chopin piece and he was magnificent! I realized then that I really was not a pianist, rather I was someone who enjoyed playing the piano and could play by ear.

Fast forward to high school, when I was asked to be a keyboard player in a rock band called "One Man Out" that played a lot of 50's music as well as a variety of rock and jazz. Again, the stigma and fear of inadequacy crept in, as well as realizing that my talent did not exactly fit into the style of music the band played. Aside from taking requests from my parents for such songs such as "I Left My Heart in San Francisco," I played the piano for my own pleasure and to enhance my own prayer experience. One time I came through for our band in kind of a big way when our band was hired for our first paying job to perform at a house party. The people attending the party were older adults and they were requesting such songs as "Alley Cat," and "I Left My Heart in San

Francisco." I was the only band member that could play such songs! It was a one-off for One Man Out, but a wonderful experience for me to heroically deliver what was needed for this event. So, when Father DiOrio kept persisting with his invitation and need for a piano player and saying that the Lord was telling him there was someone out there that could play, he finally said the words that made me know it was me the Lord was calling; he said "Please don't be afraid. Come forward and be a blessing to all of us. The Lord wants to set you free."

My aunts confirmed this by their prodding, saying "you know how to play the piano…maybe it's you!" I found myself stand up. Father DiOrio instantly saw me stand up and he said emphatically "Yes… you." I was terrified! But I kept walking forward. He pointed me to the empty piano bench and simply said "Play." I asked, "What should I play?" He said, "Whatever comes to you." So, I just started to play. I have to admit that as soon as I clumsily got out the first few notes, I began to feel the Lord's peace settle on me and on Father DiOrio, and on those attending. As soon as I finished one song, another popped into my head, and I played it. A few times he turned to look at me and gently smiled and nodded saying "keep playing." It was so tender and beautiful; such a sweet release of the music that God had placed inside me. I think I played for 2 hours straight, until the end of the service.

It was such a beautiful experience, until it was not, when I remembered why I was there in the first place. Part of my reluctance to go up and play the piano, besides the obvious fear of failure, fear of an audience, and sense of inadequacy, was that I did not want to "use up" my cousin's miracle. Now, I don't think I really believed that God counts or doles out a limited number of miracles per service, per family, but it was in my human nature to worry about that possibility. I did not go to the healing service to be healed of my lack of belief in myself regarding using my unique gift of playing the piano; I went to the healing service to bring my cousin to be healed of blindness. I felt selfish and even embarrassed to have been the one to receive a healing that day. Yet I knew in my heart and could not deny that I was indeed called forward and set free by playing the piano that day, and that I had a gift to share from the Holy Spirit regarding playing the piano. I would love to believe that because I shared my gift, that Father DiOrio was able to call forth more healings that day.

When the service ended, we all went home peacefully, silently, and exhausted. My cousin was not healed, but amazingly he was not depressed and went home peacefully, moved by what he experienced that day. My cousin and my aunts were overwhelmed by the power of the healing service, as they had never been to such a service or witnessed healings. I will never understand how the Lord chooses which healings will be released and to whom at a given time. As for me, I was "blown away" as they say.

And it did not end there...

Years later in 1989, I found myself in a new parish that I was visiting for the first time. I could not believe that at the end of the service the music ministry leader made an announcement to the congregation saying, "our piano player will be moving to Florida for the winter, so we need a part time person to play the piano at the 11:30 mass during the winter months." Is there anyone who could serve? I found myself raising my hand, a total stranger to the parish who was just visiting that day! I ended up hired to play at the 11:30 mass for several years, every winter, until the parish eventually hired a full-time music minister. It worked out perfectly because I did not want to be committed to a particular mass and schedule during the summer (I was in my early thirties and enjoyed going to the beach on weekends) and I was not an early riser, so 11:30 am in the winter was perfect for me, and for the other pianist as well.

My cousin is completely blind as of this writing, and it continues to be my fervent and heartfelt prayer that he will have a miraculous healing in his lifetime. Even more, he would say, pray that we find a cure for RP so the healing would be for many, not just for him. He grew up to be a truly remarkable person and leader in the community, influential, successful, dynamic, a powerful force of nature to be reckoned with…he is a Parks and Recreation Director and an advocate for the handicapped and has been the catalyst for making changes to empower those with disabilities to have equal dignity and ability to function to fulfill their life's purpose; all done with a great sense of humor and a deep faith. He likely would not have accomplished so much for so many without the cross he carries.

We are called to trust that God sees differently than we see, and to know that He sees everything.

What About Your Story?

Have you ever felt guilty for your blessings, when loved ones seem to be struggling and you have so much?

Are you able to receive with gratitude and joy God's blessings and healings when He seems to be saying "It is your turn to receive"?

The Gift of Being Named

I hesitated to include this memory, because it is intense, and beyond my ability to explain theologically or rationally. I invite you to read it as an account of something I both experienced and observed. I share it as a miraculous moment because I cannot deny that something real happened in the spiritual realm that seemingly has manifested itself as healing in the physical realm. I will provide you some background for the sake of context.

My mother's mother had eight children, but the eighth baby, a boy, was delivered on the way to the hospital. He arrived at the hospital as a healthy baby, but someone at the hospital cut the umbilical chord too short and he bled to death. My grandmother was never the same after that. Not only because she lost her baby son, but because the Catholic church at the time would not allow her to bury her son in a Catholic cemetery with his Catholic family members because he died before he could be baptized. She was not even allowed to have him baptized in the Church "retroactively." A Protestant family friend offered her one of their family grave plots, and my baby uncle was buried there with a stone that simple read "Baby." I cannot imagine how the Catholic church could have taken such a position, and my grandmother lived the rest of her life not only grieving the loss of her son, but also with the fear that her baby could possibly not get to heaven. Many years later, in 2007, Pope Benedict XVI changed the church's teaching regarding what happens to unbaptized babies. He did away with the place called "Limbo." It was too late for my grandmother, but I am grateful others will not have to suffer the way she did.

Over the years, I noticed that there were issues in my mother's family with having children, particularly with having sons. I am a believer that when things are not right in the spiritual realm, problems can manifest in the physical realm. Also disturbing to me was the manner in which my grandmother passed. She had some kind of liver disease which affected her rational mind. She was the type of person that was always as meek and gentle and quiet as a baby lamb. When we went to see her, and got off the hospital elevator at her floor, we would hear her moaning and crying out from down the hall. It sounded like she was saying "Oh Ma" ...over and over again. The nature of her illness caused her to bleed continuously through her nose, ears, and mouth. My sister, who is a much better nurse-like caregiver than I, kept wiping the blood from her face. It was horrifying. I could not help but recall the birth of her eighth child, and that he had bled to death, and I wondered if there was some strange connection to that event going on.

Lest this entry get too creepy, I will jump ahead to after my grandmother's passing. Days after she died, I kept having a dream that seemed very real to me. In the dream I kept seeing her face and especially her mouth forming a name – she kept saying to me "John." I do not know how, but I instinctively knew that she was talking about her son who had died. I asked my mother if my grandmother had named the baby and she vaguely remembered the name was going to be John if the baby was a boy. His Protestant tombstone only said "Baby."

Also interesting related to this dream was that there was a Catholic priest named Father John Hughes who had a ministry of healing the family tree. He conducted masses post-death to administer sacraments to the deceased. Given the intensity of the dream that I had, I made an appointment with Father Hughes to talk about my dream, and my grandmother's history with the Catholic Church concerning her baby. Fr. Hughes said he would offer a mass where my family would be invited to attend, and during the mass he would name the baby (in effect baptize him) and dedicate his soul to the Lord (in effect a funeral service). We scheduled the mass. I hesitated to invite all my mother's family because they already thought we were "over the top" religious fanatics and I could not imagine explaining this at the time. It ended up being my mother, my sister, and my Aunt Peggy (who was my mother's sister, my grandmother's caregiver, and my godmother) that attended. All I can say is that I had such an amazing peace after that mass was offered, acknowledging this person in history that was my uncle. I realize how superstitious this may sound to you, my reader, and as I said already, I really can't explain or defend the theology of it all. All I know is that I believe that after this mass was said, my grandmother could rest in peace, as could her son, John.

This experience caused me to remember the scripture verses from the Book of Isaiah 49: 14-16 when God says:

"But Zion said, "The Lord has forsaken me, the Lord has forgotten me.""Can a mother forget the baby at her breast and have no compassion on the child she has borne? Though she may forget, I will not forget you! See, I have engraved you on the palms of my hands...."

My grandmother surely never forgot the child she had borne, even if Mother Church could. But better still, the Lord God will never forget.

I was honored to be able to be there in the church when my baby uncle received his name, John. And I knew that the power of the name of Jesus broke whatever curse had been placed on our family. I am happy to say that three of my sister's four daughters have each delivered a healthy boy as well as some of my cousins on my mother's side.

Through this experience I also learned the value of, and the gift that is, our name. Being named at birth is a birthright, and at our baptism, a sacrament. Our baptism is meant to seal our name and our identity in Christ. And then for those of us who make our confirmation, we take on a new name, the name of a saint that we somehow relate to or admire. Many of us probably just remember getting something like a new watch or a cross necklace (or money in an envelope if you are Italian!) for our confirmation gift. We probably do not recall that we received a sacrament intended to release the power of the Holy Spirit more fully into our Christian lives. And we often forget why we chose the confirmation name that we chose, or worse, we forget the name itself!

There is power in a name, in God's name, and in our name.

In Isaiah 43:1 God says to each of us:
"I have called you each by name and you are mine."

What About Your Story?

Are there tragedies in your family history that still need healing or closure?

Were you ever wounded by the Church?

If so, ask God to heal that wound. Ask Him to lead you to someone who can help.

My 30-Day Retreat...Come Away with Me

In my experience, "another wound" equates to "another mistake." And each new mistake necessitates a need for healing.

I got married in 1986 at 29 years old, and not to the handsome man I passed in the hallway. Perhaps I panicked as my 30s were fast approaching and friends kept telling me I might be "too picky" or "too religious." I will spare you the details of the over-the-top 1.5-year courtship where I was on a pedestal, which led to the 1.5-year marriage where I went from the pedestal to becoming the mother my (ex) husband hated. I found myself in a classic abusive marriage. I filed for divorce in 1987, after spending most of our marriage in marriage counseling. I sincerely tried to save (or rather create!) my marriage but I knew enough from my counseling training to know that abusive relationships only get worse, and family and friends were concerned for me. After this three-year period, I knew that I needed healing, and I desperately wanted to understand how I could have allowed this marriage to happen to my life when I had been so careful all through my twenties to wait for the right person.

That was the wound. Now let me tell you about my healing time-out.

As well as knowing I needed healing, I wanted a time-out to analyze what happened so I could prevent such a thing in the future, as well as to seek discernment for the rest of my life's purpose and dreams. The last thing I ever thought I would be, or ever wanted to be, was a divorcee - a Spirit-filled Catholic Charismatic Christian divorcee at that, as that certainly seemed like an oxymoron to me. I was afraid to take one more step without inserting a great big pause into my life.

Part of the curriculum for Pastoral Ministry at St. Joseph College had included training to become a spiritual director, which focused on St. Ignatius and the Spiritual Exercises. Without writing too much about that, suffice it to say that part of the spiritual exercises involved making a 30-day silent retreat. The retreat was for the purpose of getting away from all the distractions in one's life to get quiet and listen to the many voices clamoring within. The goal is to be able to discern more clearly which inner voice is God's voice, to find direction for one's life given one's life circumstances, and to discern one's calling or purpose. It is important to pay attention to our inner patterns and movements – in Ignatian terms the guidance is to look at patterns of consolation, desolation, temptation, desires, and grace, which are usually best understood by observing and then reflecting on them. Reflection also includes paying attention to dreams which are often a time when God can speak to us, because our controlling mind is asleep. The retreat also considers discovering and acknowledging one's God-given gifts as they become apparent.

One of the greatest gifts I ever gave to myself was to go on this 30-day Ignatian *silent* retreat. I know that 30 days of silence sounds overwhelmingly daunting, even a little bit scary, but the truth is once you are silent for about three to four days, you begin to hear the inner voice in your own heart as well as God's soft whisper. It's uncanny the transition that occurred when I turned off the outside noise to listen to what my inner self wanted to express and reveal to my conscious mind.

I was not sure what to expect but what I hoped was that I would leave the retreat in a better frame of mind and spirit than when I came in.

So, I entered the retreat as a single divorced person, a little less than one month after my divorce was finalized. I entered with the expectation that this time away would be time well spent. I wanted to seek love and guidance from my relationship with the Lord.

It is important to realize that the 30-day retreat is not a counseling session; in fact, you need to be reasonably well balanced psychologically to go on the retreat, as 30 days of silence requires a seasoned prayer life to realize you are not alone, and the retreatant needs the ability to be alone without becoming despondently lonely. In addition, every retreatant is assigned a spiritual director that you meet with for one hour a day. So, being on a silent retreat is not the same thing as being in solitary confinement! It is so calming to get away and tune out many of the voices that clamor for your attention. That is when you can begin to hear the still small voice of God who wants to speak truth and love to you, and gently show you your own often hidden desires. God often leads through the desires of our hearts that He has placed there. When we get in touch with the desires we have, God can then lead us toward the path we are called to be on, which is the one we long to be on. We need to listen to those desires and find out what they are trying to tell us about ourselves and our purpose. I think that we are often as afraid of our own inner voice as well as imagining what God's would say to us.

Consider this scripture from 1 Kings 19:11-13:

"The LORD said, "Go out and stand on the mountain in the presence of the LORD, for the LORD is about to pass by." Then a great and powerful wind tore the mountains apart and shattered the rocks before the LORD, but the LORD was not in the wind. After the wind there was an earthquake, but the LORD was not in the earthquake. After the earthquake came a fire, but the LORD was not in the fire. And after the fire came a gentle whisper. When Elijah heard it, he pulled his cloak over his face and went out and stood at the mouth of the cave."

God's voice was as gentle as a whisper. Similarly, our inner voice is not the thunderous voice of our anger, or the shattered voice of our emotional earthquakes, or the fire of revenge, but is rather the gentle prayer that follows once we can finally speak honestly to God, trusting in His love, acceptance, comfort, and peace.

I was accepted into the 30-day retreat I had applied for at Campion Renewal Center in Concord, MA. I was assigned a wonderful and seasoned spiritual director, Fr. Jim Bowler. Every morning after breakfast I would meet him at 8:30 for about a 45-minute daily session. Not only was the retreat to be silent, as in not talking to other people except for the one hour a day appointment with the director, but it was also silent in the sense of not reading books, unless the director suggested one based on his discernment as to how the Lord seemed to be leading me. The idea was to eliminate distractions away from God's direction. Even good thoughts in good books can be distractions. I could also bring a Bible and a journal to write in. Every day at the morning session I was asked how my day and evening went, how I was experiencing my prayer times, and how I related to the Scripture reading that I had been given – what were my reactions, thoughts, what part especially stirred me, etc. Sometimes I was given several readings, and then asked which one I resonated most with. I was also asked what I thought God was saying to me in those prayer times. That input and my response the next day provided the director an idea of what he might assign next.

There were no phone calls either, but I could write and receive letters (this was back in 1988 so we did not have cell phones and texting and emails). Even written correspondence could be a distraction, and I found that at first it was comforting to "stay connected," but then as the retreat progressed, I did not want to be too involved in what was going on outside of my limited sacred time alone with the Lord. There would be time enough for all of that after "re-entry" into the world I had temporarily left behind. It cannot be overstated that the purpose of the retreat was to be as open as possible, and to come in with as blank a slate as possible, to allow God to guide during this time.

The ride over to get to the retreat was so much like my life! I was carefully pointed on the right road then spaced out a bit and did not know which way to go. This was before GPS's were in our cars. I ended up lost in Boston, took a road, went the wrong way down a one-way road, did a U-turn, and spotted a sign for Route 20 W! So, I just stayed on it and somehow got to the retreat center.

After I arrived, my retreat began gently and cautiously...I first found my room; then the women's shared bathroom that was assigned to me and a few other retreatants on my floor; the chapel; the room where I would meet with my director; the prayer room; the cafeteria; and the beautiful grounds and gardens outdoors. The prayer room was a separate room that was arranged to be a comfortable place to pray when you did not want to stay in your room or go outdoors, having comfortable furniture as well as floor pillows. There were not a lot of distractions but a few key symbols that were there to facilitate uncluttered and focused prayer, e.g., a crucifix, a few inspirational paintings, and a Bible. To be honest, even though I had studied the Ignatian spiritual exercises, I did not know what to expect for my own situation, or how I was going to handle the experience. I wanted to keep things comfortable and familiar, to start slow, so I decided to first take a walk outside.

Just as God finds a way to speak through dreams, imagination, and scripture, He also finds a way to speak through nature, which was also part of my retreat experience. To my delight, that first late afternoon I met a rabbit, hopping around freely in the lovely garden, and he became a friend of sorts. I especially enjoyed when he thought he was hiding from me by ducking his head under a plant, while I could see his cottontail the whole time! He was a sweet presence and if there was a day that I did not see him I felt a tinge of loneliness.

Later at 5:00 pm daily mass, there was a reading from Isaiah 55 – "my thoughts and ways are not yours" that spoke to me. I wrote in my journal for the first time: "I wait, Lord, for you to surprise me. I am not sure specifically why I am here, or what I expect...healing, wholeness (so the fragmented feeling would change), integration (of all the "me's"), vision and affirmation that you are indeed with me on this journey that I am now on. I need to understand better why I married the person I did, and I need a sense of self. Lord, I need you so much. I miss you and need to be here for a long time. I need time - to rest - to rest in and with you..."The other words at mass from Psalm 63: "the mouth of the liars will be silenced." That also spoke to me as I was seeking to better discern deception, particularly, self-deception.

I realized very soon that the important tool on this retreat was keeping a daily journal; actually, it was more like an hourly journal. What I mean by that is, we were given a Scripture verse to pray with that day, and we could pray and structure our time as we felt led. Being a more flexible person, I would pray, and then write in my journal any reactions I had to the reading, or inspired thoughts about it, and then I would take a break and go outside or get in my car and drive to Walden Pond or Marlborough Beach. I often chose to forego lunch to "play outside" instead. I had a lot of freedom within the structure of the retreat to plan my own time. I had to be back for daily mass at 5:00 pm, followed by dinner. The retreatants would all dine in the same room but at separate tables, and we would smile or nod to one another, respecting not just the rules but the CHOICE we all made to be silent so we could hear God better. We prayed for each other.

The journal was hourly in the sense that throughout the day a thought might come into my mind, and I would want to jot it down to reflect upon later. We were told to observe nature too because God also speaks to us in nature. So, if something moved me, I would write it down, or, if I had a detailed and intense dream at 3:00 am, I would get up and write it down as well. God speaks to us in our dreams too in a symbolic language that is often in symbols because it rolls out of our subconscious. Once we sense the symbols our dreams tend to use, we can begin to interpret them with the help of the Holy Spirit who "explains" them when we are psychologically ready for the truth they are revealing. I learned that the quieter I was during the day, the louder God spoke to me at night! My dreams became quite vivid, and informative, and they worked with my imagination to bring me healing not only from my divorce, but from a lifelong of set of patterns that most likely affected my ability to choose freely and wisely for my life.

During this retreat, I began to realize how much I was wired to please those around me. I never learned how to listen to my own inner voice, or even know what my own desires were. Not only did I want to seek the Lord for healing, but I also wanted some answers not only to my own actions and choices, but also to theological questions I had wrestled with. The miracle of this retreat was that I learned above all else we can bring ANYTHING and EVERYTHING to our God and He will meet us exactly where we are, as we are, and that His presence brings peace even if specific answers elude us. Sometimes God must change our questions before His answers will ever make sense.

Two scripture verses come to mind:

Luke 11:9-13 "So I say to you: Ask and it will be given to you; seek and you will find; knock and the door will be opened to you."

Proverbs 3:5 "Trust in the Lord with all of your heart and lean not on your own understanding. In all your ways acknowledge Him and He will direct your path."

And now via the next three chapters, I invite you to share memorable scraps from this life-changing retreat.

What About Your Story?

Can you recall a time when God invited you to take a "time out"?

If not, might He be inviting you now?

Is there a way that you can make time for some kind of time out for yourself with God?

I heard a preacher share this and it has stayed with me over the years. Sometimes we feel like God is so far away, and even worse, that He is not there.

But if we make a little space for God in our lives, this is what happens....

We go from:

God is nowhere.

to

God is now here.

Author Unknown

My 30-day Retreat...The Gift of Being Renamed

Before I share an experience on a farm that found its way into my 30-day retreat, I first need to tell you something about my name.

My parents named me Susan Marie when I was born. My mother's real name is Mary. I often wondered why at my birth she did not give me her name for my middle name. At the time of my confirmation, when it was time to choose a confirmation name after a saint that inspired us, I asked her about the choice of my middle name. She told me that she gave me the middle name Marie because it was the middle name of my godmother. That at least made sense to me - I always look for a logical reason. But my feelings about it never went away, so when I got divorced and went before the judge to take back my maiden name (and life!), I changed my middle name to Mary. I became Susan Mary Ceraldi on May 9th, less than one month before I began my 30-day retreat.

One day early in the retreat during one of my free afternoons, I took a ride and noticed a sign for a nearby farm. I decided to turn in and visit some farm animals. As I wandered around the farm, I walked inside a barn where I saw what looked like an aquarium tank and it had baby chicks in it, peeping away. Their cheerful peeping demonstrated such an energetic enthusiasm about being alive, and it made me smile. I could not help noticing how "new" looking they were, with fluffy, clean, and soft light-yellow fuzz. My eyes then wandered above them, and I saw a sign above the tank that said, "Born May 9." I immediately got goosebumps because that was the date of my divorce and my "new" name!

The next morning when I met with my spiritual director, he asked me how I spent my free day and I mentioned the farm, and the baby chickens that hatched on my divorce date. I thought it was kind of silly to think much about it, but he told me not to ignore such seemingly small things, because God speaks to us in many different ways. To me, those newly hatched chickens were a sign of my new birth. And so far, Susan Mary did not have much of a past to contend with, and she certainly had the promise of a new life ahead.

Names are important. Consider how parents-to-be look through name books and often say "we picked out a few, but we are going to wait until we see the baby before deciding on a name." And look how deliberately we choose a name for our pets! Our name is somehow a reflection of who we are at this moment in time. I remember in *Les Miserables* the prisoners were identified by a number, not a name. Removing their name stole their identity and destiny.

When speaking about Jesus, and His name, Luke writes in Acts 4:12: "Nor is there salvation in any other, for there is no other name under heaven given among men by which we must be saved." That is why we pray in the Name of Jesus.

We also find in scripture times when God gave a person a new name later in life after they acted in faith. Probably the best-known example is found in Matthew 16, when Jesus renamed Simon to Peter, which means the "Rock," after Simon proclaimed that Jesus was the Christ, the Messiah, the Son of the Living God. Here is the scripture:

[13] When Jesus came to the region of Caesarea Philippi, he asked

his disciples, "Who do people say the Son of Man is?"

14 They replied, "Some say John the Baptist; others say Elijah; and still others, Jeremiah or one of the prophets."

15 "But what about you?" he asked. "Who do you say I am?"

16 Simon Peter answered, "You are the Messiah, the Son of the living God."

17 Jesus replied, "Blessed are you, Simon son of Jonah, for this was not revealed to you by flesh and blood, but by my Father in heaven. 18 And I tell you that you are Peter, and on this rock I will build my church, and the gates of Hades will not overcome it."

In the Old Testament God renames Jacob to Israel in Genesis 35:9-10 after Jacob wrestled with an angel, got a dislocated hip, but prevailed:

9 After Jacob returned from Paddan Aram, God appeared to him again and blessed him.

10 God said to him, "Your name is Jacob, but you will no longer be called Jacob; your name will be Israel." So he named him Israel.

Hence, the Israelites, and modern-day Israel, were named as well.

Sometimes, when we go deeper in our prayer life and listen for God to speak, we begin to hear Him in a way that is unique to our personal relationship with Him. Sometimes we discover that God has a special name for us, a nickname if you will, like the way that we have endearing names for one another.

The important takeaway is this: our name means something to God.

What About Your Story?

Do you like your name?

Do you know why your parents gave you the name they chose?

What does your name mean? e.g., my name Susan is of Hebrew origin and means "lily."

Try asking God what nickname He might have for you.

My 30-Day Retreat...the Shells

"Inner healing" is a term used to describe the healing of memories, or wounds we incurred over our lifetime. Some of these wounds could have even occurred in the womb. This type of healing involves prayer first and foremost, and belief in the resurrected Jesus, who is alive and well and still healing His people. Along with prayer, dreams and the imagination can also be used by the Holy Spirit to help us "re-enter the scene when the event occurred," only this time with Jesus present in the scene, in order to experience healing from that memory. It is amazing how the imagination can picture Jesus, and the scene unfolding; however, this time, with Jesus present, healing happens, because the Holy Spirit transforms the scene into a healing moment. In this chapter, I will demonstrate this theory by sharing one of my retreat experiences.

One of the theological concepts I was struggling with on this retreat was the question, "Who is 'Mother God?' if there is a Father God, and His Son, Jesus?" The teaching about the Triune God of our Christian faith is that God is Father, Son and Holy Spirt. Not Mother! In my Roman Catholic up-bringing Mary was offered as Mother God. But that never sat peacefully with me because Mary was merely human. We were also taught that the church was our mother, "Mother Church." My logical engineering mathematical mind needed equivalency in the Godhead; if there is Father God, then I needed to find, or understand why there was not, Mother God. Somehow through this prayerful questioning process, the Lord showed me a deep wound in myself that needed to be healed, regarding my relationship with my mother.

Let me say that sometimes we have wounds because they were truly caused by another person, but sometimes we have wounds due to a misperception of a wrong done to us. It almost doesn't matter if it really happened or was perceived as happening, because the effect is the same: a wound exists, either way, and it needs to be healed. Many of my wounds had to do with *my misperception* of what was going on in our family's life. I think that Jesus tells us to forgive others "no matter what" because, yes, in many cases they have truly hurt us; but there just might be times when we were hurt due to our own misunderstanding or lack of capacity to understand at a young age. It is good to learn this lesson and it helps make forgiving a little easier.

My prayer times resulted in insights that were profound and unexpected. I found myself remembering when my sister was born, and the rejection I felt when my mother was in the hospital for a long week after her second C-section delivery. I had never been left with a babysitter before this, and in fact I spent some of her pregnancy in bed with her because she needed bedrest. As a result of such time, our bond became even closer.

My maternal grandparents, and my single aunt who was also my godmother, took care of me during that time. Even though I was in a loving and safe place, I ached for my mother, and I was afraid that I would never see her, or my home, again. My father came by every day after work and had supper with us, but then he would leave from the dinner table to visit my mother (and the new baby, who I did not yet realize existed.) I talked to my mother on the phone every day, but my comprehension of the situation was sparse at best, because I was still only two years old when my sister was born. When it was finally time for me to return, my aunt and grandmother drove me home. My mother, who could not wait to see me, greeted me at the door, overjoyed to see me! However, there was one little problem for me…she was holding another little baby girl! I was so confused and disoriented. My mother later told me that the first thing I said to her when I first saw her was "Did you get new wallpaper?" followed by "Is my bedroom still upstairs?"

My emotional upset continued when my mother got up in the middle of the night for feeding times with my baby sister. I wanted to get up in the middle of the night and be part of those times with her, and not be left out! In her understandable fatigue and exasperation, she would send me back to bed to go back to sleep. As a result, I bought into the misperception that I was "being replaced." I began to gravitate toward my father as the nurturer in my life. My mother, as a stay-at-home mom raising us, became the disciplinarian, even though she was the one that cooked, fed us, and kept us and the house clean. My image of God became firmly established in my mind as "Daddy."

Quite unexpectedly, this early childhood struggle of mine entered my retreat experience. I was very surprised that instead of working on my failed marriage, which I thought was my biggest issue, the Lord had me focusing on my relationship with my mother. In hindsight, God clearly wanted to heal me of wounds resulting from my misperceptions, and to restore the reality of my relationship with the loving mother I always had. I had a profound prayer time, where the Holy Spirit used my imagination to the degree that I "saw" the Lord Jesus bringing me to His mother, Mary, to heal my perceived mother wounds by embracing me as the daughter that has always been loved and irreplaceable. I saw her embrace me, tell me I was a beloved daughter, and that I was irreplaceable. She then brought me to my earthly mother, who reached out to embrace me as well.

I am not saying that Mary is Mother God, or that I fully understand where my prayer journaling led me. God affirmed to me that Mary is indeed the mother of the only begotten Son of God, Jesus (I do believe that gives her some major clout in the motherhood department...) and the Holy Spirit had me picture Jesus sharing her with me. I have since come to believe that the Holy Spirit is the "Mother God" that I was looking for. (Interestingly, the Hebrew word used for the Holy Spirit in the Old Testament is "ruah" and means "breath" or "air," and the word's gender is feminine!)

After that intriguing yet exhausting prayer session, I decided to drive to Marlborough Beach because my favorite way to unwind is at the ocean. After settling down for a while, I decided to walk to the water and put my feet in. At that moment a wave washed up, and then went back out to sea, placing two large shells at my feet, one at each foot. The shape of the shells was astounding to me, given my prayer time: one shell looked like a female breast and the other was a more elongated shell. "Mother and Father God-shells," so to speak. In this case, as is often the case, God doesn't always directly answer our questions; however, He does find a way to let us know that He heard our questions and that He is present to us as we search for answers. The shells "told" me that God was listening.

Photograph by Susan Jaquith

I still have these shells to this day, on my nightstand, as a reminder of just how present God is to our every wound, our every question, and our every thought.

What About Your Story?

Has God ever directly answered a question or prayer soon after you expressed it?

How did that make you feel?

Is there a question or memory you would like to talk to God about now?

Ask Him to answer you in some specific way that will help you know God heard you, even if the answer is not yet forthcoming.

My 30-Day Retreat...God's Throne

This moment of the Lord's gentle but clear intervention occurred during one of my prayer times toward the end of my 30-day retreat, when God used my imagination to show me something about myself. I described it in my book "Scraps from the Father's Banquet Table: Spiritual Food for Thought," Part 3, Chapter 6 "Surrendering to God – True Freedom, on page 138:

"Surrender to Jesus as Lord. Jesus is our Savior, because of what He did for us by surrendering His life on the cross, giving us the great gift of Salvation. But He is not always our Lord – He only becomes our Lord when we make Him that in our lives – when we surrender our lives to Him. Who sits on the throne of your heart? I remember being on a retreat and using my imagination to try to "picture" my heart. I saw an image of my heart...it was a room with a huge throne in it, and on the throne was this little girl swinging her legs, twirling her hair thinking and saying "I want this...I want that...ooh look over there...wow! Look at that!" And I saw Jesus kneeling on the floor, looking up at the little girl (me). My heart broke...Jesus my Savior on the floor? Why was Jesus on the floor? In my imagination I saw myself slowly slip off the throne and lower myself down to the floor. I looked down, kind of ashamed, and I motioned for Jesus to sit on the throne, where He belonged. And you know what He did next? He scooped me up and put me on His lap! That imagery has stayed with me for years, because it showed me how I needed to allow Jesus to be not only my Savior, but my Lord."

God made it quite simple for me to understand when I saw the "spoiled brat" version of myself on the throne. Perhaps if I did not get up off that throne right away in my imagination, and give Jesus His seat back, God may have had to give me a less subtle image on a second go around! I am happy to say that I did not need a second image or go around, because I was appropriately recalibrated after seeing my self-centeredness the first time. The Lord is so kind and gentle. He reveals truth to us one moment at a time, lest we break.

I could not help but recall when Jesus stooped down to wash the feet of His disciples at the Last Supper. Just as the disciples became uncomfortable with that, especially Peter, I felt that awful discomfort by the image of Jesus stooping in front of me. I am often surprised that Jesus allows us to put Him where we choose to put Him in our lives. The amazing thing, though, is that when He is on the throne in our heart, that is when He is most free to bless us and provide for our needs even more so than when we are the ones calling the shots.

Christians believe that Jesus ascended into heaven to take His rightful place on His throne at the right hand of God, the Father. In the Book of Revelation, John describes several visions of seeing Jesus, the Lamb of God that was slain, sitting on His throne, surrounded by angels worshipping at His feet. What a contrast these biblical images of God's throne are to the one God showed with me on the throne! I clearly saw that I had not yet surrendered my all to God. I was quite content having Jesus attend to my every need, never realizing until that moment that I was still the one calling the shots. I wanted all that

God could give me, but I had not really thought about my response to God's love.

Like the Kingdom of God, the throne of God is eternally in heaven, but is also here now, in every human heart that lets Jesus in when He knocks. Mysteriously, it is also yet to come. In the Book of Revelation, Chapter 21 verses 3-5 we are given a very specific image of the throne of God and a sense of the absolute authority of God.

> [3] And I heard a loud voice from the throne saying, "Look! God's dwelling place is now among the people, and he will dwell with them. They will be his people, and God himself will be with them and be their God. [4] 'He will wipe every tear from their eyes. There will be no more death' or mourning or crying or pain, for the old order of things has passed away." [5] He who was seated on the throne said, "I am making everything new!" Then he said, "Write this down, for these words are trustworthy and true."

God will always be on His throne in heaven no matter what we think, do, or believe; we can never remove God from His throne! The question that remains, though, and the point of decision for us is: who sits on the throne within your heart? When God is not sitting on that throne, there is a sense of emptiness and longing in your heart for God. When you invite God to sit on the throne of your heart, you become aware that you have immediate access to His presence, His guidance and words of wisdom, His protection, and the comfort and peace of being able to climb up and sit on His loving lap. It is that intimacy with God that every human heart is longing for.

I left the retreat much stronger, and more whole than I'd ever been in my life. After the retreat, I began the process to obtain an annulment of my "mistake" marriage. The annulment brought me closure, further insights into how I ended up in such a marriage, and hope for a second chance. I learned that my relationship with God had to come first in my life, followed by taking appropriate care of myself, before a healthy marriage could happen. I am reminded of the quote (Author unknown):

"I looked for my Friend, but my Friend I could not see,

I looked for my Self, but my Self eluded me,

I looked for my God, and I found all three."

What About Your Story?

Who do you sense is on the throne of your heart?

There is another story that I once heard that reveals our self in relation to God. It goes like this:

Imagine yourself driving in your car along the highway of your life. You see Jesus on the side of the road. What do you do?

Do you drive by or pick Him up?

If you pick Him up, where do you put Him:

Driving the car?

Riding in the passenger seat?

In the back seat?

In the trunk like a tool or spare tire in case you need Him?

Where have you put Jesus in your life right now?

A Petite Miracle about a Petite Baby Grand Piano

This is a petite story about a petite miracle about a petite baby grand that made beautiful music and a very big difference in my life.

As I described in Chapter 12 "God Sees Differently than We See," I first started playing the piano in kindergarten. I took piano lessons for several years on a used upright piano that my parents could afford which was kept in the basement because of its size. After they were certain that I was serious about practicing and sticking with it, my parents gave me a wonderful surprise gift...they bought me my first brand new piano...a beautiful walnut spinet that fit nicely against the living room wall without taking up too much space. I think I stayed up until 2:00 am playing one song after another. I could not believe it was mine, and that I no longer had to go down to the cellar to play. To this day having a piano is an important part of my life.

While on my 30-day retreat in 1988, I journaled about someday buying a real baby grand piano. I remember thinking that I could not imagine fitting one into my one-bedroom apartment, or ever having the funds to buy one. But it was one of those things I wrote in my journal as a "someday desire." (That, and to someday live by the ocean!)

In 1989 I was finally able to buy my first home, a two-bedroom condo. I was so excited to finally have my own place! There was so much room compared to the one-bedroom apartments I used to rent. I thought that maybe I would buy a piano but wasn't exactly sure where it would fit. I was very dismayed when I saw the price tag of a new piano.

One day I was having lunch in a restaurant with a friend, and I saw an adorable "mini grand" piano. It was shiny black, and I just fell in love with it. When the waiter came to the table I said "I love that piano! Do you know what kind it is?" He said he would ask the owner what kind of piano it was, and that he knew the restaurant owners wanted to sell it and were planning to auction it off the following week! I learned that it was called a petite baby grand. It had an almost square footprint of 5 feet 2 inches deep and 5 feet 2 inches wide. Because of its shape (it tapers from the width of the keyboard to a rounded point), it could wedge perfectly into the corner of my living room, taking up less space than a spinet would need because a spinet would need an entire wall. A new petite baby grand at that time cost a little less than 6 thousand dollars. I put in my bid for $1800.

After I put in my bid, I heard stories from people cautioning me about buying a piano from a restaurant or a lounge. The concern was that there would likely be cockroaches in it! I would never have thought of such a thing, and the fear did not really stick with me. I figured I would deal with cleaning it if I was fortunate enough to "win" the auction.

A few weeks later I got a phone call that I was the only bidder for the piano, and that if I would up my bid to $2000 the piano would be mine. I was delighted! I said a little prayer asking Jesus to cast out any cockroaches, then bought the piano. I enjoyed that piano gift from the Lord for many years, moved it once from the condominium to a new colonial home that my husband and I had built in 1997, and sold it finally in 2019 well after we both retired and sold our home to downsize.

And I am happy to say, there was never a cockroach to be found. Even a petite miracle shows you how big God is, and how He cares about and orchestrates both the big and the small details of our lives when we ask Him.

Photograph by Susan Jaquith

What About Your Story?

Do you recall ever having a wish just miraculously come true? And you wonder, if I hadn't been in that place or with that person at that specific time, it would not have happened!

Did you thank God for giving you this gift?

Miraculous Healings – 1990

Over the years in the charismatic renewal, I learned a lot about healing; and yet, at the same time, I learned that we cannot really understand the gift of healing on this side of heaven. As always, the real lesson is that we are not God, and He decides what is best, and He sometimes chooses to work through us at His bidding. If He needs us to do something to help build His kingdom, then He will empower us for the task. I love the expression "God doesn't choose the anointed, He anoints the chosen." Being empowered, or anointed, never means that we are God. Rather we are tools in God's hand, and the gifts of the Holy Spirit are tools that He gives us to continue the ministry of Jesus in our time in history. Allow me to get into "teacher mode" for a moment...

At first when I experienced the baptism of the Holy Spirit, specifically, receiving the gift of tongues, I thought that perhaps healing automatically came with the package. It does, only if it is God's will to heal someone through you! All the gifts are subject to the will of God. I came to understand that the gifts of the Holy Spirit were not given to the Christian church to entertain us, or as a reward for being holy. Rather, the gifts of the Holy Spirit were given as tools to build up the church to help get the word out that God sent Jesus to save us. We often forget that without Jesus's death and resurrection, there would be NO WAY back to the Father. With that said, I will get back to my story of miraculous healings.

In 1990, my father was diagnosed with stage 4 colon cancer. This terrible news came to us shortly after his company Emhart was bought out by Black and Decker, and he had to choose to retire early or move to South Carolina. Dad was 62 years old at the time. He had opted to take an early retirement but was afraid of the financial impacts, and he had made so many financial decisions "betting on" long life. So, when he was faced with the stage 4 cancer diagnosis, he felt he had made bad decisions for what he anticipated would be his surviving wife.

He had surgery to remove the malignant tumor that was causing bleeding and the inability to get through a meal at the table without having to run to the bathroom. Fortunately, the tumor was in a location that did not require a colostomy bag; however, all four of the lymph nodes that the surgeon biopsied were malignant (hence the confirmed stage 4 diagnosis.) He had to have chemotherapy once a week for the next year after the surgery.

My father has always had a great sense of humor. We talked about saving his hair when it fell out so that we could make him a toupee. He even thought that perhaps we should start on that sooner than later, by collecting his hair after every haircut until there wasn't any more hair to collect!

Because of his desire to have our family close together in the unknown time he had remaining with us, he immediately booked a family vacation to Florida on the beach so we could be together and go to Disney World. His focus was on us, and he freely shared his fears and love with us.

Our family was part of a weekly charismatic prayer group that we all attended regularly for fifteen years when this cancer diagnosis happened. After each hour-long prayer meeting, there was a healing prayer corner available at the end of the meeting for anyone that wanted prayers either for themselves or loved ones. My father got prayed over every week and we called it his "spiritual chemo treatment."

There were two Bible passages that we were drawn to and that we prayed when we prayed over my father. The one I found was from the gospel of Mark 16:15-19:

> [15] He said to them, "Go into all the world and preach the gospel to all creation. [16] Whoever believes and is baptized will be saved, but whoever does not believe will be condemned. [17] And these signs will accompany those who believe: In my name they will drive out demons; they will speak in new tongues; [18] they will pick up snakes with their hands; and when they drink deadly poison, it will not hurt them at all; they will place their hands on sick people, and they will get well."

> [19] After the Lord Jesus had spoken to them, he was taken up into heaven and he sat at the right hand of God. [20] Then the disciples went out and preached everywhere, and the Lord worked with them and confirmed his word by the signs that accompanied it.

It was the words "when they drink deadly poison, it will not hurt them at all" that I prayed related to his having to "drink" the deadly poison of chemo.

The second reading was a psalm that my sister was drawn to pray for him, and she asked him to pray it every day:

Psalm 91
> [1] Whoever dwells in the shelter of the Most High
>   will rest in the shadow of the Almighty.
> [2] I will say of the LORD, "He is my refuge and my fortress,
>   my God, in whom I trust."

³ Surely he will save you

 from the fowler's snare

 and from the deadly pestilence.

⁴ He will cover you with his feathers,

 and under his wings you will find refuge;

 his faithfulness will be your shield and rampart.

⁵ You will not fear the terror of night,

 nor the arrow that flies by day,

⁶ nor the pestilence that stalks in the darkness,

 nor the plague that destroys at midday.

⁷ A thousand may fall at your side,

 ten thousand at your right hand,

 but it will not come near you.

⁸ You will only observe with your eyes

 and see the punishment of the wicked.

⁹ If you say, "The LORD is my refuge,"

 and you make the Most High your dwelling,

¹⁰ no harm will overtake you,

 no disaster will come near your tent.

¹¹ For he will command his angels concerning you

 to guard you in all your ways;

¹² they will lift you up in their hands,

 so that you will not strike your foot against a stone.

¹³ You will tread on the lion and the cobra;

 you will trample the great lion and the serpent.

¹⁴ "Because he loves me," says the LORD, "I will rescue him;

 I will protect him, for he acknowledges my name.

¹⁵ He will call on me, and I will answer him;

 I will be with him in trouble,

I will deliver him and honor him.
¹⁶ With long life I will satisfy him
and show him my salvation."

During that one and only year of chemotherapy, my dad did not lose one strand of hair due to the treatment, nor did he lose his appetite. After receiving his weekly treatment as an out-patient at Hartford Hospital Harry Gray center, he and my mother would go out for a steak dinner to keep his immune system strong. He refused to give into the fear or buy into the expected dreaded symptoms. Although he did get weaker, the only sign I saw in his physical body was a weakening and blackening of his nails, and a darkening of his skin color. That is how we knew he was really receiving chemotherapy and not a placebo!

After completing the full year on chemotherapy, he was cancer free. Of course, he had to get tested every three months for five years after that before he could be pronounced completely free of that cancer. As of this writing, dad is alive at 95 years old, living in his own home with my mother who is 93. I know that he was healed.

Also at that time in our prayer group, another woman had been diagnosed with breast cancer for the third time. She received a healing as well and is still going strong in her 90's. My father went on to survive prostate cancer treated with radiation pellets, two occurrences of a benign pituitary gland tumor affecting his vision, both requiring sinus surgery to remove, and open-heart surgery in his 80's – complete with a triple bypass and a pig valve replacement. Since I drafted this book he had an emergency but successful hernia surgery in his small intestine at age 95. He is our "poster child" of miraculous healings!

At the time of my father's colon cancer surgery, there was yet another healing that I believe I witnessed, one that is much harder to explain, let alone prove; but when I think back to it, I do believe that healing power was being released from our prayer group into the places God was sending us, even beyond the circumstances we were aware of. Here is that story.

When my dad was having his colon surgery, my work colleague's son was riding his bicycle and was hit by a car. Back then, helmets were not required. He sustained serious head injuries and was life-starred to Hartford Hospital. His brain was swelling. I received a phone call from my co-worker the night it happened, asking me how my father was, and asking me to pray for his son. My friend was told that his son would never lead a normal life, including even being able to eliminate bodily waste on his own. He would need care for the rest of his life, and he was still a young man in his early teens. The fact that he called me asking for prayer for his son was in itself a miracle, in that my friend considered himself to be an atheist, more precisely, a scientist, and we had often had somewhat passionate discussions about faith and religion. A particular memory comes to mind. I had a pro-life poster in my office depicting a professor posing a situation and then a question to his class. It went like this:

A professor in a college ethics class presented to his students with a problem. He said, "A man has syphilis and his wife tuberculosis. They have had four children: one has died, the other three have what is considered to be a terminal illness. The mother is pregnant. What do you recommend?" After spirited discussion, the majority of the class voted that she abort the child. "Fine," said the professor, "You've just killed Beethoven!"

Source: *Tale of the Tardy Oxcart*, page 2

Every morning when I came into work, I saw that someone had covered up the name "Beethoven" and replaced it with the name "Attila the Hun," then "Hitler." I would remove the bad name to return my poster to its original message. One day I came in and my poster was torn into pieces and left on my chair. He saw me picking up the pieces and admitted to me that he was the one that had been tampering with the poster because he hated it and that it made him angry. So, when he asked me to pray for his son, I knew that his asking for prayer was coming from the depths of his soul, mixed with much fear.

The next day, after visiting my father, I decided to walk to the part of the hospital where my friend's son was. I hesitated because I knew it was certainly not a suitable time for visits. But the prompting of the Holy Spirit propelled me there. When I got to his room, I did not even go in. Instead, I stood in the doorway, observed him, and began praying. I raised my hands facing him and I prayed quite a simple prayer: "Lord Jesus, please heal this young man. My friend cannot handle this." Within a few days my friend told me that his son had taken a turn for the better, and that against all odds he was regaining faculties they thought he would not be able to regain. He went on to live a normal life.

I will never understand how the gift of healing works, but I can never deny the fact that the miraculous power of God is poured out at times through us, and we cannot control when or how it is released. There are no magic words or incantations. We who believe in Jesus are called to pray in the Name of Jesus for the Father's will to be done in the situation we find ourselves witnessing, and to pray with Scripture when the Holy Spirit brings a Word from Scripture to our attention. We do not see the entire situation or the impact this sickness has on the person's spiritual life, or on others that are in that person's life, so we must trust and continue to have the faith that when we pray, and ask, God's power is released into the situation even if it is released in a way that is not the immediate healing we want to see.

And there is no denying, sometimes miraculous healing is released according to "our will," when our will is aligned with God's, and that brings great joy.

"...for I am the Lord that healeth thee." Exodus 15:26, King James Version

What About Your Story?

Has God ever healed you?

Have you witnessed God healing someone else?

Do you ever pray for God to heal you?

Do you ever pray for God to heal someone else?

Do you believe that God still heals today?

Our Wedding Date

Here comes a good part of my life, with miracles of rejoicing, when I got engaged to marry that handsome man that I passed in the hallway almost ten years prior! As I said in the dedication of this book to Bob, he was and continues to be one of the greatest miracles of my life.

After a short courtship (given our ages and the almost ten years that passed since we first saw each other in the hallway) we decided to marry. Planning a wedding is always a stressful but exciting time in a couple's life, and we very much wanted to have a real wedding to celebrate our finally found real marriage.

One day we were driving around Watch Hill, RI, which to us was every bit as magical and idyllic as Newport, RI, with a casual elegance that we just loved. Napatree had become our favorite beach at that time. It was natural, uncrowded, and the waves were gentle. The first glimpse of the ocean coming into view when walking up the sand dunes from the parking area to the ocean was something I would pay money for (we did, come to think of it, parking fees were quite expensive!) as the view was breathtakingly beautiful.

As we were contemplating where to have our wedding we drove around the block and lo and behold I saw for the very first time, a simple white chapel simply named the Watch Hill Chapel. It was perfect, one that dreams are made of. We parked the car because I wanted to see if we could go inside and see it. God had it planned for sure, because the caretaker just happened to be in the parking lot when we pulled in, and he allowed us to go in and get a peek inside. Although raised a Roman Catholic, I have always appreciated the way the Holy Spirit worked in my faith life through other Christian denominations. It was the Billy Graham crusade that got me to take my first deliberate step towards Jesus, and the multi-denominational prayer meeting at the Tufts chapel that continued to expose me to other Christians from a variety of denominations, including the Messianic Jewish woman that brought me to my first Catholic Charismatic prayer meeting. When I walked into the chapel, I saw the words above the altar: "There are many waves, but one ocean." It was a chapel used by several denominations. I immediately knew in my heart that this was where I wanted to be married. The caretaker told us we had to call the Town of Westerly to obtain permission to book the chapel. We had had June 21st in our mind as our traditional "Saturday wedding in June," and to our great joy the chapel was available on that date!

Behind the chapel was our favorite restaurant, the Watch Hill Inn. It was perfect. You could simply walk to it from the chapel to get to the reception there. We contacted the restaurant, the minister, the photographer, the limo, the florist, and the cake maker. To our delight again, all were available on June 21st, which I was told was a miracle right there given the short notice of our planning (months, not years!)

We were just about to order our wedding invitations when I got a phone call from the Town of Westerly that a Watch Hill resident needed the chapel on June 21st, and the way it works is you can rent it IF no one else in Watch Hill needs it. Unbeknown to us, we could be bumped! And bumped we were. Everything just tumbled down with that one phone call and at that point it was getting close to the month of June. What kept bothering me was that it was the chapel that I felt so strongly about. I did not want to pick another church or chapel.

So, I started the phone call chain, leaving panicky messages when I could not get a real person to answer, and trying the next, then the next, then the next...Finally I reached a real person, and it was our photographer. I explained that our June 21st date had fallen through and asked what he had available for the summer, and if possible, in the month of June. He almost laughed; except he knew I was quite distraught. He said, "Well, I think I am all booked up through the fall but let me check my calendar. To his surprise, and my further angst, he said I only have one Saturday available. It is on June 6th! I panicked because that was two weeks sooner than June 21st which was already an aggressive date to meet. I asked him to hold it for me "in case," and that I would get back to him once I heard from the others.

Long story short, every one of our suppliers had June 6th available. It was uncanny! We did not have to look for anyone new. So, we booked our wedding for June 6th which meant that I had to start looking for a gown in April! It was too late to order one, and it was a matter of finding one on the store rack that I liked, and that fit, and that I could afford. Again, another miracle...I found a dress on the rack that only needed some minor alteration.

For the bridal party, I found a lovely fabric that was floral (periwinkle and peach flowers) on a white background and had the maid of honor's and bridesmaid's dresses made from it. I found a dress for our flower girl, also on the rack and the perfect size, that was a solid periwinkle satin that matched the fabric perfectly. Of course, the guys merely had to rent tuxes so that was doable even if the wedding was in a week!

Everything came together perfectly.

One day as we were driving again into Watch Hill we passed a beautifully landscaped front yard on a high hill, with the most beautiful flower garden cascading down the hill. The hill tapered down to a flat grassy area…yes, a perfect place to stand in front of the hill for wedding pictures. At that time (1992), we only had phone books, no electronic searches. I just knew that this was the spot, and I was determined to find out how I could get permission to use that front lawn for our pictures. I wrote down the address of the house, went home and began painstakingly reading the phone book until I found the address. When I found the address, I was delighted with myself! Nancy Drew would have been proud of me, too. However, being the shy person that I am, I wondered, now what? My determination overcame my shyness, and the fear of the finality of hearing the homeowner say "no." I got up the courage to make a cold call, and a woman answered who was so kind! She immediately said an enthusiastic "yes!" and told me that many others have knocked on her door in the past to ask her the same question. Apparently she enjoyed having so many people admire her garden and want to take their wedding pictures there, and it gave her joy to see the lovely wedding parties appreciating her garden. Yet another gift from the Lord to us.

When we told my husband's mother what our date was going to be, she was startled and excited. Unbeknown to us, June 6th was the date that her brother got married, 50 years ago, and she and my father-in-law were married the day after. They had a double wedding and honeymoon. We could not believe we had stumbled onto such a sacred family date. Bob's aunt and uncle had a beautiful marriage for 50 years, and again unbeknown to us, she had colon cancer likely already at our wedding. We had a special anniversary dance for them at the wedding and all my husband's family was there. It was a very special time for the Jaquith family. We learned of her cancer shortly after our wedding, and she passed before we could see her again.

Also to my surprise, when I looked at our calendar, I discovered that Pentecost Sunday fell on June 7th that year. Pentecost is the feast day of the coming of the Holy Spirit upon the disciples after Jesus's ascension to heaven, when the gift of tongues was first given to believers as a sign of God sending the Holy Spirit. It meant so much to me that Pentecost was part of our wedding date.

And yes, June 6th is also D-Day, which was another special day because the war was so much part of my husband's early childhood years. His father was away for the first four years of my husband's life.

I wish I could say we had perfect weather that day...perhaps we had used up our allotment of wedding day miracles! I woke up on June 6, 1992 to a downpour that seemed like Noah's flood. Rain was pouring down and I thought "oh no! how can this be?" Our wedding was at 11:00 am at the chapel; thankfully the rain stopped around 9:30 am. Because it was a bit cloudy, our wedding pictures came out nicely because no one was squinting into the sun. But it did not matter; we were married, knowing in our hearts that the Lord had gone to great lengths to commemorate our union as husband and wife.

What About Your Story?

Did God ever change things that you so carefully and deliberately had all planned out?

How did that make you feel?

How did it turn out?

"Meeting" my Father-in-law

This miraculous moment occurred shortly after we got back from our honeymoon. First let me digress and share that our honeymoon was not quite as miraculous as our courtship and wedding day had been because it poured all 7 days of our time in Bermuda. We could not spend one day on the beautiful beaches of Bermuda! That meant eating out and drinking more often than we had planned. The majority of those that were staying at the hotel chose to eat an early dinner at the hotel's happy hour, which usually included free chicken wings. During one happy hour, while sitting at the bar with other very disappointed and upset travelers, one of them said, in order to make us all laugh, "If I eat one more chicken wing, I will be able to fly myself home!" But I digress... back to the miraculous moment I am writing about in this chapter.

My husband's father had his first heart attack when he was only 39 years old, and then he had a fatal one when he was 53 years old. I never got to meet him.

One early morning, around 5:00 am, I was awakened by a lingering dream; you know, the type that takes a while for you to come out of, and when you do, you are not sure if it really happened or if it was a dream. The dream I had was about my father-in-law. I dreamed that he came into our bedroom to bless us while we were asleep, and I woke up looking at him as he was leaving our room, with his face still turned in our direction. Somehow in the dream I knew it was him, and in an interesting way, I woke up feeling as though I had finally met him. I think I whispered "hello".

I tossed and turned after fully waking and I noticed that my husband was awake too, which is unusual as we are both later risers. I asked him, out of the blue, "Do you ever sense your father's presence?" He was quite taken aback by my question, and he just looked at me and said "I can't believe you just asked me that! I woke up and for a moment I thought that I *smelled* my father. He always wore this certain after-shave lotion, and I woke up smelling it in the room."

Now, scholars and theologians and psychiatrists can debate this until the proverbial hell freezes over and will come to several conclusions. But for me and Bob, this moment was a loving blessing from a father that we never got to share our married life with; and rather than try to analyze it, I share it here as one of those miraculous moments in our lives.

What About Your Story?

Did you ever sense God bringing closure to unfinished business in a relationship with someone that has since passed?

Lay-Off Day

During a difficult period in our nuclear engineering careers, my husband Bob (who was the supervisor of a large engineering group that I supported but was not a member of) learned through the "loyal grapevine" within our organization that our Division President had selected our group of about twenty engineers to be laid off. This president was a businessman, not an engineer, and he had no idea what our group did for the company (this is sadly typical, I know). He also did not grasp that there were several other divisions outside of his immediate organization that would be badly affected if our group was suddenly eliminated. Bob became our hero that day – he made the rounds, informing all the divisions that we supported of the rumored upcoming lay-off decision. Quickly during that week, the rumor escalated, becoming more than just a rumor; someone had actually seen the presentation slide that showed our group being laid off *later that day*!

Bob was never the type of manager to call extraneous meetings, but he called an emergency one that day and we all went to it, quite concerned by the urgency of the call, and even more when seeing his alarm and sadness. He shared with us what was likely to come that day. It was a very strange day in that it was hard to continue working after that meeting…I mean do you rush to finish what you are working on that day, or is it a waste of time to continue working? And of course, the shock of it all affected our productivity and emotions, even if we did decide to keep on working. We went from fear to denial in that I am not sure we believed it would really happen because we knew how busy we were and how successful we had been as a supporting group, and still were. I suspect that was partly what contributed to the cluelessness of our President – when your group is in a support role it is often overlooked how vital that support group is to the success of the company…the typical unsung heroes' song…

But here is when the miracle happened…are you ready for it??? At 3:00 pm that afternoon we were all suddenly informed that the President was *fired*! Can you imagine our relief and subsequent joy?

This account makes me recall the book of Esther in the Old Testament. Esther was chosen to be queen by King Xerxes after an edict had gone out to search for a new queen. Esther was a Jew, and quite beautiful. Her cousin Mordecai who had raised her told her to conceal her Jewish heritage so as not to negatively influence the king's decision. The king was taken by Esther's beauty and chose her to be his queen. There was a man named Haman who was a highly ranked official in the king's court, and he hated the Jews, especially Mordecai, because Mordecai would not kneel before him and pay him honor. Mordecai subsequently learned of a plot by Haman to destroy all the Jews, and he brought this to Esther in hopes she could speak with the king and prevent this annihilation of her people. The king of course did not know about Haman's plan, nor did he know that Esther was a Jew. Esther fasted and prayed to seek from the Lord a plan to reveal this conspiracy to the king. With great courage she appeared at the king's inner court, without invitation. This was courageous because to approach the king's throne uninvited resulted in one of two possible outcomes: either she would be killed for this act, or the king would invite her to approach the throne with her request. The king chose to invite her to approach and make her request. She made a request to host a banquet for both the king and his nobleman Haman. Haman was delighted, relishing the belief that he was quite important and highly favored. Before the banquet, he continued with his plan to destroy the Jews, starting with Mordecai, and had a pole erected on which to impale Mordecai the next morning. When Esther exposed Haman's plan and wickedness at the banquet, the king ordered Haman to be impaled on the very pole he intended for Mordecai.

Bob was our Esther. And we all got on our proverbial knees, Christians, Jews and atheists alike, recognizing the miracle of that day that could have "impaled" so many lives, as well as the success of our business.

Psalm 59 became our song!

It's a bit long but I didn't want to delete any stanzas at the risk of losing the power in the prayer when read in its entirety.

Psalm 59

1 Deliver me from my enemies, O God;

   be my fortress against those who are attacking me.

2 Deliver me from evildoers

   and save me from those who are after my blood.

3 See how they lie in wait for me!

   Fierce men conspire against me

   for no offense or sin of mine, Lord.

4 I have done no wrong, yet they are ready to attack me.

   Arise to help me; look on my plight!

5 You, Lord God Almighty,

   you who are the God of Israel,

   rouse yourself to punish all the nations;

   show no mercy to wicked traitors.

6 They return at evening,

    snarling like dogs,

    and prowl about the city.

7 See what they spew from their mouths—

    the words from their lips are sharp as swords,

    and they think, "Who can hear us?"

8 But you laugh at them, Lord;

    you scoff at all those nations.

9 You are my strength, I watch for you;

    you, God, are my fortress,

10 my God on whom I can rely.

    God will go before me

    and will let me gloat over those who slander me.

11 But do not kill them, Lord our shield,

    or my people will forget.

  In your might uproot them

    and bring them down.

12 For the sins of their mouths,

    for the words of their lips,

    let them be caught in their pride.

  For the curses and lies they utter,

13 consume them in your wrath,

    consume them till they are no more.

  Then it will be known to the ends of the earth

    that God rules over Jacob.

14 They return at evening,

    snarling like dogs,

    and prowl about the city.

15 They wander about for food

and howl if not satisfied.

16 But I will sing of your strength,
   in the morning I will sing of your love;
  for you are my fortress,
   my refuge in times of trouble.

17 You are my strength, I sing praise to you;
   you, God, are my fortress,
   my God on whom I can rely.

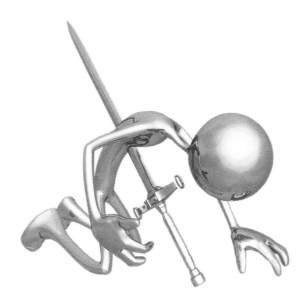

What About Your Story?

Has God ever done an instant Rescue in your life?
If not, do you need to ask God for one now?

Finding a Needle in a Haystack

My husband was born in Newton, Massachusetts, and at the age of 4 years old, he and his family moved to Rutland, Vermont where they lived until he was 12 years old. After his father had his first heart attack at 39 years old, his family had to move hastily in a rather drastic way due to the fact that his family was evicted from their rental home because the landlady was afraid that she would lose her rent because his father could no longer work. She already had a new tenant lined up.

During those years of my husband's childhood, he had made some close friends that he had to abruptly leave without saying goodbye, not to mention they had no time to find a place to live. This resulted in the temporary plan that for a time, required his family to split up – his youngest sister went with his parents, who stayed with friends, his middle sister went to live with their paternal grandparents, and Bob the eldest went to live with his aunt and uncle until they eventually were reunited in Massachusetts when they were finally reestablished in their own home.

Fast forward several decades later, my husband and I liked to take annual trips to Vermont to see the leaves turn, taste, and buy some great cheese and maple syrup, and drive by his old childhood home-stead in Rutland. Bob would reminisce and recall some of his favorite boyhood escapades and tell me stories about his friends that lived in the neighborhood, and in particular, his friend next door.

After a pleasant day of exploring and tasting, we went back to our Bed and Breakfast, and I noticed he was looking through the phone book. I asked him what he was looking for, because he was quite intent, and he said that he was looking to see if any of his childhood friends still lived in the area. It was like looking for a needle in the haystack, but the tug was in him to search. He did not find anyone. I felt disappointed for him even though he seemed to give up on it quicker than I could. It touched me so much that I began to pray about it, asking the Lord to help us find someone if there was anyone still there to be found.

The next day we were driving and leaf-peeping, taking in the beautiful foliage. I felt hungry for some of that great Vermont food, and soon saw a sign for a breakfast place...a pancake place! Now, anyone who has ever been to Vermont knows there are a bazillion such signs! (And anyone that knows me knows that I never miss a restaurant sign!) I said to my husband "I want to eat at that place, it looks like it will be good, and it is not too far up ahead." Since we were already staying at a Bed and Breakfast, it did not make sense to go somewhere else for breakfast, so we decided to wait awhile and save the Vermont pancake breakfast meal for dinner. On our way back that evening we found the restaurant and went inside. We were seated up in a loft on what I believe was the third floor. The restaurant was very big and open, and you could see everything below from our table on the third floor.

Halfway through our meal, my husband stopped eating, stopped looking at me, and was staring intently at the entrance door. About a minute or two later, he put his fork down, and said "I'll be right back." I assumed he was making a trip to the restroom. When he did not come back right away, I looked down and saw him talking with someone. It turned out that the owner of the restaurant that we had randomly chosen was his childhood friend, the one that lived right next door to him in Rutland! That was incredible! But even more incredible to me was that the way that my husband recognized his friend after so many years...he recognized him from the *back* of his head, not his face, because of the unique hair pattern on the back of his head, so he recognized him from a distance and from behind! It was a nice opportunity to catch up, find out about what happened to some of the childhood gang, and to explain why the family left so abruptly almost 40 years ago. And to say a proper goodbye.

This was such a personal example of how close the God of the big universe really is to each one of us. He knows how many hairs are on our heads, and He cares about everything we care about. He bothered to bring closure to some unfinished business in a young boy's heart, and to answer a loving wife's prayers.

From Matthew 10:30: "And even the very hairs of your head are all numbered."

What About Your Story?

Can you recall a time when you allowed yourself to wander, or the freedom to follow signs or tugs in your heart, or a fanciful whim?

Where did that journey lead you?

Did you find something or meet someone?

Did you find yourself where you wanted to be?

A Gift that Keeps on Giving

When I found the charismatic prayer group in Newington, CT, I found someone who was to become a spiritual pillar and dear friend in my life, Berthe Gagne. As I mentioned in Chapter 11, Berthe was the founder and one of the leaders of the prayer group, which began with five women around her kitchen table and then moved to the basement of the church, subsequently growing to about 50 people.

I was in my early twenties when I met her, at a time I was getting over some real hurts and bad choices in my life. Berthe was in her late 40's when we met. She had a tragic event in her life that made her faith in God even more remarkable to me. Berthe's husband had been killed on the side of the road after being struck by a vehicle when he stopped to help someone who had broken down on the side of the highway. She was three months pregnant with her fourth child when he was killed, and the accident happened on Good Friday. I graduated high school with her youngest, who I always knew did not have a father, but I never knew why. She never remarried and she raised four children on her own.

Berthe and I shared a deep devotion to Good Friday and Jesus's passion. Our relationship began with her as a spiritual mentor and minister of healing to me, then over the years she became more like a spiritual mother, and then a dear friend. She made me some wonderful dinners and afterwards, we would pray together in her living room. Berthe lived alone and had a ministry praying with many people one on one for healing in her living room.

Berthe had a spiritual director who was a nun and an artist, Sister Mary deLourdes, who created a powerful image of Jesus on the cross. The print was of Jesus's head bowed with the crown of thorns upon it, and His upper torso with His right arm stretched and taught conveying the pain of the constant pulling of His muscles. Sister Mary made ten of these prints, simply titling it "Love," and Berthe's print was numbered "6/10." The focal point of the print was the face of Christ. Berthe hung this framed print over the fireplace in her living room, (the room that we prayed together in.) It was a powerful image, and sometimes we would just look at it before we prayed. It always reminded us that Jesus willingly carried our sorrows and our sins, and still does. We would also pray for other people, not only for our own intentions.

Berthe had two sisters who suffered from Alzheimer's disease who she lovingly visited and cared for. Once when we were having lunch in our favorite little Italian restaurant, she shared with me that she was concerned about getting forgetful. I tried to minimize her concern by saying that I too was starting to forget things. She said no, this is different. Then she took my hand and said, "I pray to God that I don't completely lose my mind." To my great sorrow and surprise, Berthe was eventually diagnosed with Alzheimer's. Because she knew from family experience just how the disease would progress, she said to me once "If I ever get angry and lash out at you, please know that I love you." She no longer wanted me to visit her, and she eventually went into a nursing home.

I visited her once at that home and was comforted by the fact that she still knew me. I sat across from her and took her hands and said, "let's pray together." To my delight she began to pray in tongues with me. I learned then that there is nothing greater than God within us, and even Alzheimer's could not steal her prayer language from her. Berthe passed peacefully in her sleep at 83 years old. She did not completely lose her mind as she feared, but she did lose being in touch with reality; for example, she thought she was in a hotel, not a nursing home, and kept saying that she wanted to go home.

After she passed, Berthe's wake was on Mother's Day weekend in May 2010. I knew in my heart that she was at peace, though the legacy of her great life, hidden from most "regular people" including her own family made it terribly hard for me to see her pass, and I could not believe this was how her life ended. So many memories flooded my mind, and I especially relived many times together in her living room. I grieved in faith and found myself saying over and over "Oh, my Berthe..."

At her wake I went through the receiving line and hugged everyone in the family. As I got to the end of the line, her youngest son, my friend from high school, called to me saying "oh Sue, come here, I have something for you." I walked back over to him, and he told me to wait a minute, that he had something I might want. He then left the reception line, went into a back room, and came out with the print "Love." He said no one in the family had a place for it, and they did not know of anyone else that would appreciate it to the extent that they would hang it in their home, and they thought of me. They were going to donate it if I didn't want it. Want it? I cherished it.

So, on Mother's Day weekend, my dear friend and spiritual mother found a way to give me a gift, at her own wake no less, years after she had lost her ability to speak coherently or make any deliberate decisions. True to the title of the painting, it was such a gift of love from my friend and from her son to me. It was also a kind of spiritual sign that gave me comfort and a deep peace – I sensed that she had indeed found her way to her heavenly place, where she is living in the fullness of joy; a place where she can now be reunited with her husband, and behold the true face of Love, Jesus, face to face.

From the Song of Solomon 8:6-7:

"Place me like a seal over your heart,
like a seal on your arm;
for love is as strong as death,
its jealousy unyielding as the grave.
It burns like blazing fire, like a mighty flame.
 Many waters cannot quench love;
rivers cannot sweep it away.
If one were to give all the wealth of one's house for
love, it would be utterly scorned."

"Love."

What About Your Story?

Think about a special item that means a lot to you. Was it a gift that was given to you or something you found or bought for yourself?

Is there a gift that you might be called to share with, give to, or bequeath to someone else?

Forgiveness in Full Bloom

I have always loved the gardenia flower. My grandmother is the only person I know that could grow one consistently for years on end, with healthy shiny leaves and large white blooms. She kept it on a table in her enclosed back porch, so that when we climbed the stairs to her second floor home the beautiful, sweet fragrance of gardenia greeted us. (Then when you entered her kitchen, you were overwhelmed with the incredible fragrance of perfectly cooked Italian food. But I digress...)

The break-up I described in chapter 7 came back to me several times in my life in that every high school or college reunion could potentially result in an encounter. It was never comfortable, but I was determined not to allow the breakup to erase all my memories and other friendships. In 2011 I received a phone call from my ex-boyfriend, telling me the tragic news that he had a malignant brain tumor. He asked my forgiveness after all those years...33 to be exact...I was on his list of people he wanted to make amends with. I was deeply struck with grief, not over losing him, as I had already gone through that a long time ago, and that was complete, and at this time I was happily married. I was struck by grief at the loss of his life at 52 years old. He had so much to live for. I appreciated his calling me as he had never asked for my forgiveness, though I told him I forgave him on more than one occasion.

About a month later, I attended a Good Friday evening service in 2011 and found myself praying for him, for God's will to be done, and hopefully for healing. On Easter Sunday I received a phone call from a mutual friend that he had passed that morning.

I did not go to the wake, as I really felt that would likely cause more tension for his widow, and I could pray for him and his family from home. However, on the morning of his funeral, I found myself feeling that I should go, and I really wanted to go...but as anonymously as possible. I did not want to go through a greeting line but imagined that I would slip into the back of the church and simply be prayerfully present.

In my home I had a gardenia plant that would not bloom. It was alive yet the leaves and buds would just drop off before they would even open. I could not figure out what I was doing wrong. The morning of his funeral I walked into our family room and immediately smelled the sweet fragrance of a gardenia! There on that plant was one perfectly formed, pure white, gardenia flower. I knew in my heart it was a sign that it was right that I go to the funeral; not only that it was right, but that I in fact belonged there. I went to the funeral and am so glad that I was there. I learned that through the years he had genuinely found his faith. At the end of the funeral service, they played a recording of him singing a gospel song. Because he was incredibly musically gifted and had used his God-given talent both professionally and in his church, it was most appropriate that he would sing at his own funeral.

Miracles are a two-way street. I believe they happen more often than we realize. Part of the miracle I experienced was my gardenia blooming for the first (and only) time. The other miracle was me seeing it, smelling it, and sensing the gentle invitation via its presence that it was time to complete the forgiveness cycle with this person in my life, and to say a final goodbye.

From Matthew 18:21-22:

²¹ Then Peter came to Jesus and asked, "Lord, how many times shall I forgive my brother or sister who sins against me? Up to seven times?"

²² Jesus answered, "I tell you, not seven times, but seventy-seven times."

What About Your Story?

Forgiveness is a decision we make, and it is more often realized in stages rather than all at once, instantly, like peeling layers of an onion.

Is there anyone that you need to forgive now?

Is there anyone that you need to forgive again?

Following the Breadcrumbs

In his book "Christian Caregiving – A Way of Life," Kenneth Haughk reminds us to reclaim our heritage as disciples of Jesus; to remember that as Christians we have something unique to offer those who need care. This is not to dismiss caregiving done by professionals, using specific techniques or best practices; rather Haughk invites us beyond those by being also open to the realm of God's intervention while we offer our care, and to the realization that in addition to some tried and true conventional methods, we also have our faith to offer. Via our baptism, we have each received the Holy Spirit and spiritual gifts unique to who we are as well as the circumstances God has placed us in.

Haughk also affirms that it is natural to be uncomfortable with the idea of sharing our faith – we are all like that. Why? Because our faith is the most vulnerable and sacred part of who we are. So, the challenge, or call, is to push through the awkwardness, and look for the open doors that allow us to naturally bring our faith into our actions of caregiving. And he says that sharing our faith should not be a monolog! It should be dialog, and there are cues people give us when they need to talk about the spiritual part of their being.

Haughk also says we need to remember that we are the caregivers… only God can be the Curegiver! What a relief that is! We are not responsible for results…God is. God gives us tools as well as gifts… from the profound to the practical…from praying with someone and sharing an inspired scripture or reading from a book, to offering a cup of cold water if that is the greatest immediate need.

A friend of mine gave me Haughk's book and asked me to read it and give a day-long workshop to the caregiving ministry at our church based on the concepts in the book. When I read Haughk's book I remembered a moment in my life where the outcome was not what I wanted, but when I still could not deny that I knew God was at work in the situation. It comes under the category of "Why God?" events, or more accurately, "Why not, God?" The following paragraphs describe what happened to me when I wanted to help a woman in my prayer group who was dying of ovarian cancer.

I first met her at my church in Connecticut after I had just made an announcement at the end of the service about an upcoming Life in the Spirit seminar that I was offering to give for the parish. She came up to me after the announcement to ask more about it. I had never met her before, and so I was quite surprised when she made the direct statement "I was just diagnosed with ovarian cancer." She also said it with a big smile and a chuckle which was disconcerting and confusing. I realize now that I missed the cue: the truth was that she really was quite afraid. I invited her to come to our monthly prayer group, where we pray with people that are seeking God's touch and healing. She started coming to the prayer meetings.

Our parish prayer group prayed over her every month for almost 5 years – she would come for her "spiritual chemo." It was the cancer journey that I'm sure many of us have witnessed or experienced – times of remission when it is easy to say "thank you Jesus" and times during chemo when blood counts are bad again…but what we did see in her was a real deepening of faith. She joined two ministries in the church

– working with kids (she could never have children) and music. She loved music and singing. She attended the prayer meeting regularly, and then at some point it was clear she was not feeling well enough to come. There was a time when we were not aware of how she was doing, and no news did not seem to be good news.

On a seemingly separate note, before giving this seminar at our parish, I had given a Life in the Spirit seminar at another parish, and they did not have a live music ministry available to support the day. Because I believe that music is an integral and indispensable part of the seminar, I made a CD of our prayer group music that I could use. I have since kept this CD in my car to use on long drives. It occurred to me that I should also give a copy of it to my friend as she had not been able to attend our prayer group. I thought she would enjoy it as I knew what some of her favorite songs were, and they were included on the CD.

The feeling to give her the CD got stronger…I felt very "led" to do it and I sensed the persistent nudge of the Holy Spirit which did not stop and only grew stronger. Sometimes the nudge is a thought that we wake up with that doesn't seem to go away until we act on it type of thing. I call it "Following the Breadcrumbs." I had no idea why I kept thinking of getting this CD to her, but I just knew I had to do it. We were told at church to keep her in our prayers and that she wasn't doing well. She suddenly went from baring her soul to us, to needing complete privacy. I inquired about her from our deacon, and he said confidentially that she was now in hospice in a hospital and did not want any visitors. I knew that I needed to respect that…but what about the CD and the Holy Spirit's persistent nudge to give it to her?

A few weeks later I was invited to breakfast at a friend's home in a town that was a couple of hours from where I live because a mutual friend of ours from Pennsylvania was coming to visit and hoped to see both of us. She had moved away and would only be back in town for a few days. On the way to her house I played my CD as it was almost a 2-hour drive and the music always put me in a peaceful and prayerful frame of mind. After a lovely breakfast with my friends, while driving home, I noticed signs for a hospital, and it was the hospital where my friend was in hospice. I could not help but notice that the breakfast meeting place was 5 minutes from the hospice hospital where my prayer group friend was dying. I struggled because I knew I was not invited to visit her, yet I had the CD in my car, and I was a mere 5 minutes from where she was. I found myself driving to the hospital just to get as close to her as I could, and decided I would just sit in my car in the parking lot and pray for her from my car. I also asked the Lord what He wanted me to do. After I prayed a few more moments a gentle thought entered my mind: "I can just go in and leave the CD at the nurse's station for her without going to her room!" That thought came with such assuredness and peace that I got out of my car and went into the hospital. I asked at the reception desk what floor she was on so I could drop something off for her at the nurse's station and surprisingly they gave me her floor number. I said surprisingly because I thought I would be told to just leave it with the receptionist. I did not ask for, nor was I given, her room number.

It turned out that her room was right next to the nurse's station and her husband saw me at the station. He turned to his wife and said, "Looks like they've found us." I was devastated and embarrassed. Not only was I not invited, but I also felt that I was not even welcome.

But she said to him "tell her to come in." So, I did.

Her loving and protective husband, said to me "you can sit with her and hold her hand but don't talk…she's too tired to talk." He then said he had to run a quick errand and asked me not to stay more than 15 minutes. So, I sat there just holding her hand and praying silently. A nurse came in so I asked if there was a CD player in the hospital that we could use.

My friend was in that semi-conscious place…she told me she hadn't finished going to all the places on her bucket list and was bummed about that. She then was quiet again…then after a time she said "can you get me a cold washcloth? I feel like I'm burning up," so I eagerly went to the nurse to get a cold pack for her, feeling that sense of relief that comes when there is something I could actually "DO" to help her.

Then the nurse came back with a CD player and put in the CD I had brought with me. I felt embarrassed again – I don't know why except that it was such a vulnerable moment and I was still unsure if I belonged there in the room at such as time as this. I certainly understand the need and right for privacy, and I had been second guessing myself for so long about what was right and what was wrong to do.

The first song played. She smiled and whispered: "I love this song," then she rested again.

Her husband returned and I promptly stood up and said that I would be leaving. I squeezed her hand and her parting words to me were "I sure hope heaven is a fun place." Everything in me wanted to reassure her that it was, but of course, how could I *know* for sure? I've never been there! But what I could say, with all my heart, soul, mind, and strength was "**I BELIEVE** that it is." I stood on the scripture verse "Eye has not seen, nor ear heard, nor has it entered into the heart of man the things which God has prepared for those who love Him." (1 Corinthians 2:9). It was then that I realized that it was my faith in this promise that was the real gift that I had to offer her, or anyone else for that matter; my faith in a God who loves us, who sent His Son to make a way for us so we will not die forever but have eternal life in a beautiful place with God called heaven. I could honestly say to her "I believe." She said, "I hope so." Those were our last words to one another.

About a week later I was at her wake. When I got to her husband in the receiving line, we hugged and he said, "That CD you gave to us…I burned it!" Not being familiar with the term "burned a CD" I at first assumed he hated it and threw it away! But then he went on to say "I could not stop playing it, 24/7; it is what got me through those last days. I realized that the CD was not only for my friend but was also a gift from God to him that he also very much needed.

I learned firsthand again how much the results are up to God. We never know which thing that we do will make a difference or bring healing to someone else. We do not know God's big picture and how God works to heal through us. But we know that He knows and has a perfect plan beyond our ability to figure out or imagine.

If you attend Christian church services, notice how many times we say, "I believe" and notice what we say we believe in. That faith that we profess is what we have to offer to heal the sick, cast out demons and share the good news with those that are seeking it.

My friend's passing was not the miracle I had wanted. I wanted to see her healed of cancer and I imagined her inspiring others with her testimony. Instead, the miracle for me was realizing that despite my lack of self-confidence or awareness of the full situation I found myself in, somehow the Holy Spirit was able to lead me through this time in a very deliberate way. I was also amazed at how perfectly correlated all these people and places had to be in order for each of us to have been in the right place at the right time. Even my friend visiting from PA on that precise weekend inviting me to meet her for breakfast in a town next to the hospital was part of God's plan.

From this experience I learned that our task is to give Jesus our "yes" to the call to care for another, and then to ask Him to guide our eyes, ears, hands, and feet, trusting that He will show us the breadcrumbs that will lead our steps to bring His love and healing where He wishes to send it through us.

2 Corinthians 1:3-5:

[3] Praise be to the God and Father of our Lord Jesus Christ, the Father of compassion and the God of all comfort,

[4] who comforts us in all our troubles, so that we can comfort those in any trouble with the comfort we ourselves receive from God.

[5] For just as we share abundantly in the sufferings of Christ, so also our comfort abounds through Christ.

What About Your Story?

Are you a caregiver to someone?

Can you see the difference between what you are able to do versus what only God can do for this person?

Can you allow yourself to feel effective doing that which you can do, even if the outcome is not what you had hoped for this person?

Can you care for yourself in this same way?

Can you follow the breadcrumbs God has scattered on your path when you sense He is leading you to some kind of open door for you to enter into someone's life?

Pray for the courage to follow the breadcrumbs.

Exiled in St. Croix

My husband and I love the Caribbean and spent almost all our vacations crashing on some island which for us was the most healing vacation known to humankind. During our working years, we tended toward Aruba because of the exquisitely beautiful beaches, and the variety of eclectic and international restaurants, many within walking distance of our lodging. After retiring we wanted longer stays in the Caribbean and had to look for more cost-effective options for long-term stays. Long-term at that point was four weeks during the coldest winter months. Friends of ours told us about St. Croix, and suggested we visit. St. Croix means Holy Cross, and as you've read in my prior entries, the Cross is the pattern of my journey. I realize that is true for every Christian, but in my life, God's fingerprints tend to reveal themselves overtly around the Cross. We visited St. Croix for several years in a row, each time staying a little longer…two-week vacations turned into two-month stays. We of course, like every other tourist, started looking at real estate. We came close a few times but weren't quite sure if buying vs. renting a property was a practical or wise financial decision, not to mention the fact that we certainly did not want to own three places at the same time. We took several vacations to St. Croix before Covid hit.

As soon as our spring vacation ended, we reserved the same condo for the fall. During the summer we were told that our reservation had to be cancelled due to a change in the property manager (a technicality in the VRBO booking system). We were told not to worry, and that our reservation would be rebooked by the new property manager. If you know anything about life in the Caribbean, we had good reason to be concerned!

Also at that time, we downsized and sold our large colonial house. It felt so good to finally have one home in one place. One morning, I woke up at 5:00 am and was so restless I couldn't get comfortable. I attributed the feeling to the fact that we had just made a huge life decision and were going to be moving some of our belongings to RI, giving some away, and leaving a lot behind for the new owner who wanted whatever we couldn't remove. But at the same time, I had this nagging thought to check my phone for real estate in St. Croix. I assumed it was related to rebooking our November vacation as that still had not happened and we were getting concerned that we would not have a place to stay. So, I got out of bed and walked downstairs, checked my phone, and saw that there was a condominium for rent and for sale in a complex that we had been considering. So, if we rented there, we would no longer need the condo reservation we had previously booked. We stayed there for the first time in November 2019 then returned to RI for Christmas and returned after the holidays with a few more back and forth trips home to see our families in New England.

In March 2020 we flew back to St. Croix for what was supposed to be a one month stay. A few days before our return flight home we received an email (not even a phone call!) that our flight was cancelled. Not postponed but CANCELLED. I tried calling the airlines and of course after waiting several hours on the phone, we could not reach a real person to talk to. I realize now they had no answers and no idea when we would be able to fly back to Rhode Island (or anywhere else!)

In parallel the Governor closed St. Croix to travelers, and restaurants were closed. It was a ghost town on an already primitive island. The good news was no one was going anywhere, or buying or selling, and we were safer in St. Croix than in Rhode Island, going by the daily Covid mortality data Bill Gates was providing. We had fresh air, as it was delightful to sit on our balcony, and I learned how to cook with whatever groceries were available on a given week. It became a treasure hunt looking for ingredients for the recipes I had googled (not to mention finding toilet paper!)

Eventually the airlines provided new flights for our return, and two more times they were CANCELLED days before we were supposed to fly home. We wondered if we would ever see our family again. Others wondered about that as well, wherever they were experiencing Covid isolation. I was particularly afraid due to the age of my parents – in their 90s and living in their home – but my sister and her family were nearby. They became their own cluster. My husband and I would call and text our families to be reassured everyone was still alive and healthy and let them know that we were ok. We could not believe the timing of all of this, and that the Lord had prepared a place for us for a comfortable Covid exile that we did not know was coming.

I remembered the Scripture where Jesus says in John 14:2 "My Father's house has many rooms; if that were not so, would I have told you that I am going there to prepare a place for you?" He was talking about heaven and eternal life, but we could not help but realize how blessed we were to have such a safe and beautiful place to be during that terrible time of Covid that was upon the entire world. It was during this time that I wrote the major portion of my "Scraps from the Father's Banquet Table: Spiritual Food for Thought" book. I am not sure it would have come together quite the way it did if not for this beautiful time of exile on St. Croix.

Yes, we often sang the theme song from "Gilligan's Island" to make ourselves laugh. And on a more serious note, I remembered how St. John of the Cross wrote the Book of Revelation while exiled on the island of Patmos.

We flew back to Rhode Island in early June, after celebrating our 28th wedding anniversary in St. Croix. We have since made St. Croix our winter residence.

I mean after all, if this was the place Jesus prepared and provided for us, why would we look for another?

"And if I go and prepare a place for you, I will come back and take you to be with me that you also may be where I am." John 14:3

What About Your Story?

This is another "follow the breadcrumbs" miracle.

Are you aware of a dream or desire in your heart yet to be fulfilled?

Can you tell if God is leading you toward or away from it?

A Rare Raffle Gift

You might be tempted to think that this entry is too ridiculously unimportant to spend time even typing it, let alone include it in a book about miracles in my life. It falls under the category of that commonly cited expression of the faithful that "nothing is too big or too small for God to care about." I will keep the typing time short, as it doesn't take too many words to describe this sweet little miracle.

Some background…my husband loves donuts almost as much as he loves me. And each year it has become increasingly annoying to him that there are no real (aka "good") donut shops to be found. He is simply not impressed with Duncan or even Allie's, as he is not interested in gooey, or frosted, or sprinkled donuts, but rather good old fashioned cake donuts that are fried for sure. He has been in search of an authentic donut shop for about 20 years now, and is willing to drive the distance to find one. He has barely been surviving on Walmart bakery donuts. Did I mention he is 80 years old?

I recently attended a charity event sponsored by the Greater South County Women's Club in Rhode Island. I bought a $25 raffle ticket that was for a wrapped bottle of wine (all I knew was whether it was red or white, but the specific type and brand was a surprise). The bottle of wine also came with a small envelope that contained a $25 gift certificate to a surprise local business. Most people at my table bought one of these $25 raffle tickets because how could you lose? You knew upfront that you were guaranteed one bottle of wine and one $25 gift certificate!

When we got back to our table, we each unwrapped our bottles and opened our gift certificate envelopes. Some women were oohing and ah-ing about their gift card – one to a restaurant, another to a café, another to a spa, another to a beauty salon, another to a sports store… so I eagerly opened and peeked into my gift certificate envelope. After a short pause, I grasped that my certificate was to a local donut shop! At first everyone at my table kindly smiled at me with that "oh, poor you…sorry" kind of smile. But then it hit me – oh my goodness!! I am holding a gift certificate to a donut shop that Bob and I had never heard of! And what if this is "THE ONE"?

I pictured coming home with my prize and kept thinking "Bob will just love this!!!" It was worth it for the joke alone, if nothing else, even if it turned out not to be a great donut shop. So, I left with my bottle of wine and $25 worth of potential donuts.

When I got home I said, "Hey Bobby - look what I won?" He was a bit surprised, and then began to google where it was located (pretty seriously actually). Well, it turned out that this donut shop was right around the corner from the church we'd been attending, so after church the following week, we found it and stopped in. Let me tell you, the smell inside the shop was amazing. Here is the other miracle within our little miracle…when I looked more carefully in the envelope to pull out our gift certificate, I noticed that there were two! We somehow had been given two $25 gift certificates to the donut shop in that envelope!

As it turned out, these were the best donuts Bob had found in over twenty years! We bought a box then returned weeks later for another, and it has since become part of our routine drive home from church.

When we get home, we make some fresh coffee and I know better than to interrupt those first few moments when my husband settles down for that first bite. It is such a joy to watch!

Do you believe how intimately God can be with us when we seek to love Him? He cannot be outdone in love and generosity! Not only does He know the number of hairs on our head, but He also knows the desires of our heart - from small and mundane, to really important and critical to our happiness. You know, I think that it is the simple miracles that really show us how infinite and all-powerful God is.

Matthew 6:33

"But seek first his kingdom and his righteousness, and all these things will be given to you as well."

What About Your Story?

What are the little things that bring you delight or joy – maybe not a donut, but something you can name and treat yourself to when possible? A walk on the beach? A day at the spa? A pedicure? A special dinner out? A day fishing or golfing?

When is the last time that you took some time to enjoy a simple pleasure?

"Taste and see the goodness of the Lord" once in a while!

The Miracle of Perspective

This chapter is a reflection on the relationship between miracles and perspective. There are two ways to approach this reflection.

One way is to consider the idea that whenever we experience a miracle, that miracle will forever change our perspective (e.g., about life, or about ourselves, or about our faith in God). It can even cause us to reevaluate all that we thought was true up until the time of the miracle, so the miracle causes a changed perspective. An example of this would be if a person that does not believe that God still heals experiences a healing, thereby causing their belief about healing to change.

The other approach is the idea that whenever we make a deliberate choice to change our perspective, we then have a new way of looking at a situation, which can then result in a miracle. Consider the proverbial glass is half full vs. half empty approaches to life. If I choose to focus on what is there for me, what I have in my glass, then I am relieved of the heaviness of longing for what is not there. Another way of saying the same thing is: "Happiness is wanting what you have, not having what you want." (Author unknown). So, this change in perspective can open the door to a miracle. The event I am sharing in the following paragraphs is an example of this second way of thinking about miracles and perspective.

When St. Paul was in prison, he wrote that he learned to be content in whatever state he was in. His perspective is profound, as evidenced by these verses from Paul's letter to the Philippians 4:11-13:

> [11] I am not saying this because I am in need, for I have learned to be content whatever the circumstances. [12] I know what it is to be in need, and I know what it is to have plenty. I have learned the secret of being content in any and every situation, whether well fed or hungry, whether living in plenty or in want. [13] I can do all this through him [Christ] who gives me strength.

The Holy Spirit gave me a simple prayer to say at those times when I find myself in a circumstance that I feel is unpleasant, and to be honest, unwanted. The prayer is "Lord, give me the 'grace to embrace' this unwanted circumstance that You have allowed in my life." Accepting the 'grace to embrace' offers us a way to transcend our circumstance, to have victory over it, if you will.

We are not asked to understand God's ways but to trust God. I am not a saint, but I try to remember this invitation to change my perspective, and I have found that whenever I choose to and am able to change it, I am released from the oppression and fear that comes from the circumstance I find myself in. Allow me to share an experience that demonstrates this point.

One morning I woke up feeling very ungrateful and all-around irritable. It certainly was not intentional, but everything that popped into my head was a negative observation. I was not my best self at all. I could only see what was wrong with everything. I felt dissatisfaction with limitations that came from being well into the second half of my life, the future looking bleak regarding unfulfilled goals, and the realization that I had run out of time to make certain life changes that one can still make at mid-life, but not long after. I felt that my condominium in St. Croix and my cottage in Rhode Island were both too small and I wished I could have one larger residence in one location because I do not relish traveling back and forth. This attitude even spilled into my spiritual life in that I was also struggling to find and belong to a church that was the right fit for me. I dragged Bob along to a variety of churches to try to find a church home. I do know about that great saying "if you are looking for a perfect church and find one, don't join it because it won't be perfect anymore!" I wanted to go home but did not know where home was.

This is when God interrupted my negative thinking with a miraculous moment. I sensed the Holy Spirit pose a question to me, which was more of an invitation: the Holy Spirit whispered, "Why don't you try praying for someone that has no home at all?" I was quickly ashamed of the audacity of my complaining when considering that question. After all the years that I have been seeking to be guided by the Holy Spirit, I was never faced with a question in such an explicit way that would have such an immediate and clear impact on me. The question had the power not only to interrupt my negative thinking, but to transform it.

Even more poignant is that I have been serving as a volunteer President of the Board of Directors of a non-profit called "Neighbors Helping Neighbors Rhode Island," which is an amazing all volunteer organization that provides free home repairs to low-income homeowners, thereby allowing families to remain in their homes. We work to prevent homelessness by repairing one home at a time. Believe me, the irony of the question was not lost on me. I was immediately jarred into a complete change of perspective. My perspective on my life changed, and I began to pray for all those who had no home at all, which then turned into a prayer of thanksgiving for the two homes that God has provided for me - one by the ocean and one on a lake. It is uncanny how we can so easily forget our blessings when we place our focus on what we do not have. That change of perspective was a miracle moment for me because I instantly shifted from frustration, grouchiness and self-pity to joy and appreciation for the life and blessings that I have. My rumination was transformed into a joyful reverie!

As if that wasn't enough of a lesson, that same day I had one of those days with my husband, with the natural tendency to focus on the things we disagree on, or on little habits that can be irritating. I sensed the Holy Spirit speak a similar word to me: "Why don't you try praying for someone that has lost their husband." That was another gut-punch, giving me a remedy for my misperception that I will never forget. By praying for someone who was widowed, my irritability immediately turned into gratitude for my husband, the man that I love so much, and the realization of all he is to me, all that he does for me, and for the gift of his life to me.

The miracle of changing our perspective by focusing on others that do not have the thing we are complaining about has the power to transform our outlook on life. Seeing with God's perspective has the power to transform such things as the drudgery of day-to-day tasks into the development of a strong faith that persists in difficult times, the ordinary into something special, feelings of injustice done to me into mercy for others, sense of lack into seeing and valuing the wealth of my blessings, and dare I say, the power to transform a sinner into a saint.

I also had a change in perspective when I stepped back and realized how petty I can be. When I allow myself to consider the big picture from God's perspective, I cannot even imagine how much God sees given the fact that He is aware of all of us, hearing everyone in this world that cries out to Him for help. Suddenly my inessential complaints became an embarrassment to me.

That is not to say God doesn't care about my needs, hopes and dreams, however small or even insignificant they may be, as is evident by what I've shared throughout this book. But sometimes we just need to put them in perspective....

What About Your Story?

Consider the circumstances you find yourself in at this time in your life.

For each situation ask yourself, is your glass half full or half empty?

How might you change your perspective on even just one of these circumstances? What might the resulting miracle look like?

Have you ever experienced a miracle that caused your perspective to change?

30

Angels Among Us

After the previous chapter on perspective, I thought this book was complete, especially since I could not recall any more moments to write about. Then the following event happened. I guess the Lord wanted one more miraculous moment to be recorded herein.

Here in St. Croix, we share one car, a Ford Bronco, which is sturdy for the bumpy roads, yet not too big for me to be able to handle. It has all the modern equipment such as a rearview camera, nifty dashboard metrics and a key fob, to name a few. One late afternoon we left our condo to run a few errands. Bob needed to go to Home Depot (his home away from home) and on the way we drove by a nail salon (my home away from home). I asked him to stop there so I could go inside and ask if they could take me, rather than me traipsing around Home Depot for the fifth time that week. I went inside and was told that they had one appointment left before they were going to close, so I took it. That could be considered a small miracle as well, but it is not the one I am writing about! I texted Bob that I got in and would be done at 6:30 pm when they closed.

About fifteen minutes after Bob drove away, he heard a loud "Bang Bang Bang," which is never a good thing. The fancy gadgets on the dashboard indicated that the rear driver's side tire was quickly losing air pressure. It dropped from 40 psi to 20 psi in a matter of minutes, so he knew he had to pull over fast. Before he could pull over safely, he had to get up and over a steep hill, and he told me later that he prayed "please Lord, help me get over this hill and pull over." He did get over the hill and was able to make a U-turn to pull over onto a patch of land next to a fence that seemed to be a safe place in the middle of nowhere. The tire pressure was down to 4 psi and then zero.

Bob got out of the car to get the tire jack and because the car was modern (and we no longer are!) he could not find the tire jack anywhere. New models "efficiently" hide such things, not to mention the fact that they no longer look like the old-fashioned tire jacks, so you wouldn't necessarily recognize it if it was staring you in the face either. As he walked around the car, a man came walking over to him from behind the fence. Because there was a small opening in the fence, the man was able to see Bob and the Bronco from the building he was in. He asked Bob if he needed some help, and for maybe the second time in Bob's entire life he replied, "Yes, I need some help."

It turned out that the man, Fred, was a professional truck tire repair contractor, and had all the right tools to repair a flat tire on any size vehicle a few feet away in his shop, which was directly behind the fence where Bob had pulled over! Fred was able to quickly remove the bad tire and he offered to plug it, but after removing the object that caused the flat tire, it was obvious that the hole was too large to be plugged. So, he installed the Bronco's spare tire for Bob.

After that, Bob went to get in the car, but found that the car wouldn't start! Bob reached into his pockets to take out the key fob and try pressing the buttons manually, but lo and behold, there was no key fob, or WALLET, in his pockets! He realized that he had left them both at the condo! The only reason the car started when we left to run our errands was because I had MY key fob with me in my purse, which was now at the nail salon!

As a result of this, Bob had to ask Fred for help once more (that makes a total of three times now in his life I'm guessing!) So, Fred drove Bob home to get his key fob and wallet. Bob insisted on paying him which he did not want, but finally accepted.

Meanwhile, not knowing what had transpired since Bob had dropped me off, I texted him from the salon that I was almost ready to be picked up, and that they were on time and about to close. Bob picked me up right on time, which he says is the real miracle of the story (He loves me and wants me to be safe.) The thought of me standing outside after sunset alone, waiting to be picked up, added more stress to his already "stress-full" situation. When I got in the car, he said "Hi." I asked him if he found what he needed at Home Depot and he said, "I will tell you, but I need a glass of wine first." We went home and I made some dinner, and I couldn't help but notice the somewhat bedazzled look on Bob's face. I did the typical me/wife thing, rattling off a bunch of questions all at once asking "What happened? Did someone hurt you? Did you get robbed? Did you have an accident? Did you hit someone?" He said, "No, no…I just need a minute to process all of this." When he told me everything that had happened, we both realized and appreciated how much God had watched over Bob, and me indirectly, every step of the way. We were also aware of how badly it could have played out, if left to random circumstance. It wasn't exactly a safe area or time of day at that point.

The next day we got the tire fixed – it did have to be patched from the inside (as you can see from the picture below, the object that Bob ran over was quite intrusive and large.) After the tire was repaired, Bob was still in disbelief as to what had happened, and he asked me if I wanted to retrace his journey and see where he broke down. I said "Sure, as long as we don't go over the spot where you picked up that terrible object!" We went a different way and ended up at the bottom of that

Photograph by Susan Jaquith

steep hill that Bob had to get the Bronco over before he could safely pull over. We continued driving and made the same U-turn and pulled over. Only on this day, the fence was closed (no opening at all) and completely covered with black tarp, so if anyone was in the tire repair shop, they would not have been able to see our car the way Fred did the day before.

And, just to make sure we didn't miss the fact that the Lord had just done a multiple rescue miracle for us, I happened to notice the road signs that we passed. In St. Croix, towns are called "Estates." As we climbed the steep hill, I saw the road sign reading "Estate Hope." As we made the U-turn where Bob pulled over to show me where he had parked next to the fence, the road sign read "Estate Blessing." And if that wasn't clear enough, all the orange barrels denoting the nearby construction were labeled "GRACE."

The next day Bob texted Fred to thank him again, and Fred's response was also a gift. He said he was blessed that he felt the Lord move him to go over and help the person that was stranded on the side of the road. Fred had a choice; we are grateful that he chose to act on the nudge God gave him to "be an angel" for someone in need...Bob.

What About Your Story?

Were you ever in a whirlwind of impossible negative circumstances that you were absolutely powerless to resolve? Did you pray? What happened?

Has someone, a stranger, ever come along to help you that you realized later God had sent to rescue you from a bad experience?

Have you ever been the stranger that was sent to help someone in need?

The Tome of the Unknown Miracle

To save you the trouble, if you do not already know, a tome is a book, typically a very long book at that. Like the Tomb of the Unknown Soldier in Arlington Cemetery, which commemorates and honors not just one soldier, but all of the unknown soldiers that died fighting for our country, the purpose of this chapter is to honor and thank God for all the Unknown Miracles that I did not write about either because I missed recognizing them at the time, or I have simply forgotten some of them. This chapter is a tribute to those miracles that we will never know about that happened in our lives; times when God's mighty hand intervened to either prevent some catastrophic event in our lives from happening, or times when He intervened to gently steer us toward a direction that we did not even realize we needed to go, or to take a course of action that we needed to take in order to fulfill His perfect will and plan for our lives.

Such times are likely too numerous to even imagine.

It is hard to prove a negative; it is easy to prove that something happened, especially in our generation where we have powerful cameras in our phones and social media to post even what we ate for breakfast! But how do you prove that something *did not* happen that might have? And lastly, this chapter is also dedicated to the miracles that prevented bad things from happening when God was protecting us from evil.

Some of these accounts are examples of family events that preceded our births. It is revealing to consider the effects of circumstances in the lives of our ancestors.

***

This is a moment in my husband's life that forever changed the history of his family. It is something some members of his family would remember if you reminded them, but it is mostly something no one thinks much about, and some are not even aware of. I will call it the Miracle of Cocoanut Grove.

The Cocoanut Grove fire was a nightclub fire that took place in Boston, Massachusetts on November 28, 1942, the Saturday after Thanksgiving. It resulted in the deaths of 492 people. It was the deadliest nightclub fire in U.S. history, and the second-deadliest single-building fire. That Thanksgiving weekend, when Bob's mother was eight plus months pregnant with Bob, she and his father and another couple had reservations to go to the club. As Bob was their first child, pregnancy was a bit of an unknown and when the baby did anything unusual, there was cause to pause and wonder if this might be the moment of delivery. During the day of their planned and highly anticipated big night out, Bob began kicking and moving around, and his mother felt sick. It was so bad that his parents decided they had better stay home and not go out that evening. It was later that night that the huge fire broke out. There was no way that the number of people that were in the building that night could get out, so most were trapped inside.

We will never know if the pregnant woman (Bob's mom) and her husband would have been fortunate enough to get out alive, or if they would have perished in the fire. But the odds were certainly against their surviving that fire. Just let your mind think about the ramifications of this for a moment. If Bob's mom and dad, and infant Bob in the womb had been killed that night, what would be the impact on the Jaquith family lineage that we know today? This is an example of an unknown miracle; a time that perhaps the Lord God used a tiny baby in the womb to not only save himself, but his parents, and his future family to come. Not to mention the other couple that were going to go out with his parents, and their family lines as well.

***

Both my husband's and my parents lived through major wartimes, as well as my husband. My husband's father served in World War II, and my father served in the Korean War. Of course, if our fathers served, so did our mothers. And my husband was of draftable age during the Vietnam War. Here are a few stories, Unknown Miracles, which came out of their experiences.

• My husband's father was in the Army during World War II, and shortly after he was born, his father had to leave the family to serve. He did not return until my husband was 4 years old, which presented a real challenge to the bonding of father and son. Because he knew how to type, he was given an office job in World War II rather than being deployed to the battlefield. We will never know the miracles this simple gift of learning to type brought to their lives, and subsequently to ours.

• In Chapter 1 "On Being Born" I described how my parents met. Shortly after my parents were married, my father was drafted into the Army during the Korean war. When he showed up to report for duty, acknowledging and accepting the call to serve his country, it turned out that there was a sufficient number of Army volunteers, but not enough men enrolling in the Marines. So, the powers that be randomly counted off men in the Army lineup, and my father was required to move over to the Marines line. My mother said that was the first time she ever saw him cry. They were separated as he was led

186

off to Camp Lejeune for the feared and infamous Marine Boot Camp. My mother lived with his parents during that time. After Boot Camp, my mother joined my father, and they lived in Camp Lejeune in North Carolina with the other military couples.

My father had one older brother and two older sisters. His parents were immigrants from Italy and the family was very poor, but they were fortunate enough to have one car that everyone had to share. Both of his sisters were enrolled in a typing class and my father was appointed to drive his sisters to their class. He figured "gee, while I am just sitting here waiting for them, I might as well join the typing class and learn how to type!" So, he learned how to type. Similar to Bob's father's experience, because of my father's rare typing skill as a male Marine, he was appointed to serve in the administrative side of the house, typing for the Marines, rather than ever having to go to the Korean battlefield. That typing class may have saved his life.

• My husband was protected from the Vietnam War. He was in Army ROTC but when he went for his pre-induction physical, because he had flat feet, he was immediately rejected. This rejection came moments after a young man who was in front of him in line, who was obviously crippled after having polio as a child, was not immediately rejected, because apparently walking on flat feet warranted an immediate rejection, but a polio survivor had to further demonstrate a handicap that would prevent him from marching. I am thankful for Bob's flat feet.

***

Another miracle in my father's pre-married life was when he was waiting in a storm for a bus. He was holding an umbrella that got struck by lightning! He felt the intense pressure from it, dropped the umbrella, which burst into flames, but my father remained unscathed. When I think of the times he almost "missed the opportunity to be my father" (ha!), I am amazed and grateful for the gift of my life that came through his life and my mother's.

***

My mother survived the flood of 1938. Her family lived directly across the street from a dike on the Connecticut River that you had to look up to see. During the flood she and her sisters were taken from their third-floor bedroom (the girls' bedrooms were actually in the attic, not really a third floor) in a rowboat. None of them knew how to swim, and they all developed a fear of the water after being traumatized, especially because one of their cousins drowned in the flood.

***

In light of contemplating the importance of our ancestries, I suspect that my pro-life views are formed in part by my family history, and by my deep belief that life begins at conception (certainly beyond all doubt with the first heartbeat), which is based on the many Scripture verses where God announces His creation of and destiny of the baby in the womb; in particular, in Psalm 139:

Psalm 139: 13-16 (translation from The Message)

[13] Oh yes, you shaped me first inside, then out;
   you formed me in my mother's womb.
[14] I thank you, High God—you're breathtaking!
   Body and soul, I am marvelously made!
   I worship in adoration—what a creation!
[15] You know me inside and out,
   you know every bone in my body;
You know exactly how I was made, bit by bit,
   how I was sculpted from nothing into something.
[16] Like an open book, you watched me grow from conception to birth;
   all the stages of my life were spread out before you,

188

The days of my life all prepared
before I'd even lived one day (MSG).

I think we may not grasp the importance of each human life to God. Each one of us is created in God's image, regardless of the persons that He used to give us our human form, or the circumstances that resulted in our conception that birthed us into the world. When I think of all the destinies that have been aborted, I grieve for such losses to God and to our world. We ask God for healing, but perhaps God has repeatedly tried to send us the curefinders. I can't help but believe that with each abortion, we have stopped the lives of those who might have been doctors that could have been able by God's grace to find the cure for cancer, Alzheimer's, and other horrible diseases; or artists, musicians, and poets; or scientists, counselors, and philosophers; or future presidents, kings, and pastors. The list goes on. We have aborted the missions of about 70 million souls in this country alone at the time I am writing this book.

**

Consider the events of 9/11/2001. There were many employees that for whatever reason never went to work at the World Trade Center that day. Call it a premonition, or God's intervention unknown to us, they would see in hindsight what would have happened if they had gone to work that day.

And we will never forget the 2977 fearless heroes and martyrs that lost their lives on that fateful day. Two words echo over the years, spoken by Todd Beamer on Flight 93 who courageously led the effort to bring down the fourth plane, preventing Al Qaeda terrorists from hitting yet another Washington, DC target: "Let's roll." We will never know how many lives were saved because of his faith, including even our country.

***

And then there are those times that we get stuck in a traffic jam, and we are frustrated and angry, then come to the scene of the accident and realize why the traffic was so backed up. That could have been us, and our car, in the accident, if we had left the house sooner, rather than being the car that was stuck in the resulting traffic jam. Sometimes we are late, sometimes we are early, but the timing of every moment of our lives is known and sacred in God's plan. And yes, sometimes it is our appointed time to die. We often do not notice those bad things that could have happened but never did happen.

So, let's give thanks to God for protecting us from things we are unaware of that He has miraculously saved us from. I suspect we will see a replay of our lives here on earth, when we are in eternity, when all will be revealed.

I am reminded of this verse in the Gospel of John, called the "disclaimer" in the series The Chosen:

"Jesus did many other things as well. If every one of them were written down, I suppose that even the whole world would not have room for the books that would be written." (John 21:25)

It is time now for me to draw the line on my story, knowing full well that there will be more miraculous moments in my future, some that I will recognize and celebrate, and many more that I will never realize on this side of heaven.

Hence, the Tome of the Unknown Miracle.

What About Your Story?

What are the stories of your ancestry? If you do not know or cannot recall, is there anyone that you can ask?

Can you think of a time when you knew that God spared you from something bad that could have happened?

What miracles are you aware of in your life?

Epilogue

Writing this book has been an experience of revolving memories and insights, presenting me with the challenge to not only record them, but to also reflect on each one as I put pen to paper. Some insights even came to me for the first time while writing my story, providing me with a new understanding that I did not possess at the time that God was touching and leaving His fingerprints on a specific life moment. Hindsight is always 20/20, as they say, and each account taught me more about what I consider a God-intervention or a miracle to be. I added the subtitle "Miracles of Rescue, Reset and Rejoicing" because I could recognize the times God intervened to rescue me, the times He intervened to reset the course my life was on, or the times He simply gave me a gift "out of nowhere" that caused me great joy and simply made me happy!

When considering miracles, sometimes the event I described was more of a miraculous moment, like a thunderbolt that suddenly changed everything, or a rescue from a situation beyond my ability to avoid or resolve. Sometimes the miracle was an insight from a dream or new thought, one that came and taught me something so profound that I knew beyond all doubt it was from God. Sometimes the miracle was a divine reset, where God interrupted my plodding along, going in the wrong direction, or in circles, or stuck in a rut, or stuck in a sin, or in an unforgiveness (aka wound) in my life, and sometimes the miracle was a simple pleasure that God found a way to provide in a somewhat unusual way.

We tend to think of the word "supernatural" when we hear the word miracle. I hope that the miraculous accounts I have described herein help you to recognize the "naturalness" and wide variety of instances of God's intervention in our lives. I wanted to share the miracles from my life story with you in hopes that it will inspire you to reflect on your own life's God story so you can begin to see just how many times the Lord has been aware of you and your life, and intervened in your circumstances when you thought you were alone. I hope these accounts demonstrate how intimately and personally God wants to be in relationship with you.

God goes to great lengths to reveal Himself to us. I think that He is delighted when we do recognize His hand, and fingerprints, on our lives and love Him in return for it. A miracle is not a magic trick done by God to entertain us. Miracles have a purpose, and that is to confirm the reality of God to awaken us to His presence in our lives. Jesus says in Matthew 28:20 "And lo I am with you always, even until the end of the world." (King James Version). The purpose of a miracle is to testify to the Truth that God is a Living God, someone who seeks to be involved in our lives and to lead us safely home to Him at the end of our earthy lives.

When I go to the Scriptures and remind myself of all the times that God intervened in people's lives, leaving His fingerprints; and more importantly, all the relationships God chose to have with the men and women He created, the "hearing" of these faith stories increases my faith that miracles are not only possible, but that they are the normal way that God has chosen to work in human lives. It causes me to ask myself, "Why would He suddenly stop now?" We need to recalibrate our way of thinking to realize that God's direct interaction in our lives is even more natural than supernatural!

I believe our faith in God has some bearing on what God can do in our lives, even if our faith at the time is small or even unconscious. We can have faith but not realize it; faith is a condition or propensity of our heart to either believe in Jesus or not. I believe that faith is often what ignites miracles into our present reality. Jesus said that He could not do any miracles in his hometown of Nazareth because of their lack of faith (Matthew 13:58).

In Matthew 17:20 Jesus says: "...for truly I say to you, if you have faith as a mustard seed, you shall say to this mountain, 'Move from here to there,' and it shall move; and nothing shall be impossible to you." We will probably never have *enough* faith on this side of heaven. Faith calls forth God's movement in our lives. This brings to my mind a story from the life of a Christian friend of mine. He was born and raised Greek Orthodox while living his childhood and teenage years in Greece. One Sunday morning when he was a little boy and did not want to go to church. His grandmother asked him "why don't you want to go to church?" He answered her "because I already have enough faith!" She said, "Oh, ok, I see," then she asked him to follow her outside. They went outside and she pointed to the mountain in the distance. She then said to him, "See that mountain over there? Well...let me see you move it!" That was one of those life lessons that not only stayed with him into his adult years but was powerful enough that when he shared it with others, it stuck; as evidenced by the fact that here I am now, writing about it forty years later!

After writing this collection of God's fingerprints on my life story, I came to appreciate the importance of our ability to *recognize* His interventions when they do happen, and the importance of *remembering* them. I remembered some of the post-Resurrection accounts in the gospels when Jesus appeared to His disciples for 40 days before ascending to His Father in heaven! That is astounding, isn't it? And a fact we often overlook or gloss over in the gospels. But what caught my attention was that most of the disciples that had followed Jesus before His crucifixion failed to recognize Jesus when they first saw Him after His Resurrection! Did He look that different from how He looked when He was with them those years before His death? Were they too conditioned and reprogrammed after His death to even allow themselves to see a "Risen Christ?"

Consider these accounts:

- Mary Magdalene did not recognize Jesus at the tomb until He spoke her name: "Mary."
- The disciples hiding in the upper room did not recognize Jesus until He said, "Peace be with you."
- Thomas did not believe that Jesus appeared to the other disciples until he put his fingers into the wounds on Jesus's hands and feet, and his hand into His side.
- The disciples on the road to Emmaus did not recognize Jesus until He stayed with them for supper and broke the bread, and said the familiar words: "Take and eat…"
- The disciples did not recognize Jesus on the shore until they threw in their nets after fishing all night long and 153 fish jumped in!

From these scriptures, it seems that for some of the disciples to be able to recognize the Risen Christ, they first had to recall a past moment where they did recognize who Jesus was, when they knew that He was not just an ordinary man. They then had to reconnect to that memory before they could believe it was Him now. Remembering their relationship with Him had to happen before recognizing Him could occur. I once heard it said that to remember is to re-member our fragmented selves, healing something that was broken in order to make us whole again.

I have often wondered why the resurrected Body of Christ retained the wounds from His crucifixion - the wounds that Thomas asked to put his fingers in so he could believe it was really Jesus. Perhaps His wounds remain so we can never forget that Jesus died for us, that His crucifixion was real, and so we will recognize him when we meet Him face to face. In the end, when I inevitably pass from this world, if many hands reach out for me, I will look for and grab hold of the hand with the nail print.

Remembering these special and sacred moments, reconnecting with them, and telling their story has been a real gift to me. My faith was strengthened in the process of documenting God's fingerprints throughout my life. My joy in the Lord was re-awakened; my joy in the Lord was re-awakened, and joy is such a real thing, so undaunted by our circumstances, bringing with it hope for our future.

None of us can predict, or even imagine, how the last pages of the story of our life will read. It is so interesting, this journey we are on with God; all that has happened and all that still lies ahead that will someday complete our life story. It is so exciting to think that at this very moment I am sitting right in the middle of a hundred "God-incidents" that I must wait to discover and watch unfold! It makes me realize how infinite is the wisdom of God, how intricate is His plan for our lives, and how integrated our life stories are.

Recall the "Butterfly Effect," which is the theory that a butterfly flapping its wings in one part of the world can cause devastating (or I like to add, life-giving) consequences in another part of the world. The origin of this effect was initially related to weather effects, but we now use the term to describe the reality that even a small seemingly insignificant event in one place or time can cause a major change in another. Another effect, the "Domino Effect," is similar. The Domino effect is about one event setting a string of follow-on events into motion. Because of my respect for the reality of both these effects, I often find myself paralyzed when trying to make any big life decision! It helps me to remember that the Holy Spirit will always be present, guiding me with nudges and thoughts beyond words.

My prayer for you and for myself is that by appreciating all the little miracles of our life stories that have brought us to this moment we call "Now," we will be able to anticipate the gift of the rest of our lives in a new way. "Now" is when a miracle can burst forth into our lives, and it will mark our past from our future.

God rescues and resets our lives not only to change the course of our individual lives, but in so doing, change the course of the world as well.

I hope your takeaway after reading this book is a deeper realization of how omnipotent and awesome God is, and that He offers to be intimately involved in your life. As Jesus told us in Matthew 10:29: "Are not two sparrows sold for a copper coin? And not one of them falls to the ground apart from your Father's will."

When you recognize God's fingerprints throughout your life, you can't help but also realize how very important you are to God!

Acknowledgments

I thank my husband, Robert E. Jaquith, who was the editor of this book. His insights and reminders to broaden the potential audience for this book were invaluable to me, providing kind and constructive feedback along the way. He is also quite a grammar and punctuation guru!

I also wish to thank my publisher, Dove Christian Publishers/Inscript Books, for guiding me through the publishing process, and for their Statement of Faith.

May this book reveal the goodness of God who loves each one of us.

About the Author

Susan Ceraldi Jaquith began serving in lay ministry in 1977, combining her faith journey with practical insights on how to live out our spirituality in the real world. She has served as a prayer group leader, facilitator of retreat days and workshops, and provided spiritual direction and pastoral counseling to those seeking to grow in their personal relationship with God. She worked as a part time counselor at Associated Counseling Professionals (ACP) in Hartford, CT from 1985 – 1995. She also served on the leadership team of the Catholic Charismatic Renewal for the Archdiocese of Hartford for over 20 years. After retiring, she served as President of the Board of Directors for Neighbors Helping Neighbors RI.

Sue enjoyed a successful 35-year engineering career as an engineer and manager, retiring from Westinghouse Electric Co. (formerly ABB and Combustion Engineering) in 2013. She is happily married to her husband Bob since 1992 and resides on the island of St. Croix in Christiansted, Virgin Islands, and summers in Charlestown, RI.

Printed in the USA
CPSIA information can be obtained
at www.ICGtesting.com
LVHW081406031223
765485LV00014B/936

9 781957 497280